LOVE AND LIFE

A COLLECTION OF POEMS

VIKAS KUMAR

Contents

Preface   *vii*

  1. My Conflicts And Conclusions   1

  2. Commerce   3

  3. Confessions Of A Salesman   5

  4. Modern Youth   8

  5. Nothing Like...   11

  6. Road To Modernity   13

  7. Valentine - A Wish   16

  8. The Colors Of Life   18

  9. Our English Class   21

10. An Evening To Remember   25

11. Teacher's Day   27

12. Love-I   29

13. Self-motivation   31

14. The Comprehension   34

15. Life   37

16. Netarhat School   39

17. Mr K N Vasudevan   41

18. My Soulmate   42

19. Tryst Futile   44

20. The Crush...   46

21. The Last Love...   52

22. Post-mortem Of Love   56

23. A Broken Heart   62

Contents

24. Beauty, Thy Name Is Woman!   70

25. Confidence   78

26. One-sided Love   80

27. Self-realisation   85

28. Success   91

29. The Lessons Of College Life   95

30. When You Ignore Me…   101

31. When You Look At Me   103

32. Friends   106

33. When You Walk With Me   108

34. Love- II   111

35. Mr Upendra Prasad   113

36. Suban   115

37. Mr R N Singh   118

38. Misconception   120

39. Tejas   123

40. Miss S…   125

41. Shobha Ma'am   127

42. Mr Anshuman Chatterjee   129

43. Mr Diwakar Mishra   131

44. Mataji   132

45. Shrimanji   134

46. The Contradiction   135

47. Dad's Daughters   137

Contents

48. Chemistry	140
49. Raksha Bandhan	143
50. Miss M…	145
51. Conclusions Of The Forties	147
52. Falling In Love	152
53. Good Boys	157
54. Love & Duty	160
55. Love And Loyalty	164
56. Men, Women & Love	167
57. Modern Indian Women	170
58. Personality	174
59. Promise	179
60. Romance	180
61. Self-belief	183
62. Knocking Of Love	187
63. Grave Expectations	188
64. The Experience...	191
65. Time & Love	196
66. Happiness	199
67. Princess Charming	202
68. Pursuit Of Excellence	204
69. Success & Excellence	206
70. Love At First Sight	208
71. Reading	210

Contents

72. Mothers — 214

73. A Father — 216

74. Lessons From Cricket — 219

75. The Farewell — 223

Preface

Dear Readers,

Poetry is a form of art; like all art, it has no final definition. After all, it's a subjective issue. The great poet William Wordsworth defined poetry as 'emotions recollected in tranquillity'. For me, poetry is not just emotions. We live in an age where every individual is fighting his or her own battle; we are all racing against time. It has always been the vocation of artists to find the solutions to life's myriad problems. So, for me, poetry is—Beauty and brevity of thought.

We can't deny the presence of the heart, as we are all feeling beings. Sometimes, the heart overpowers the mind, and we are immersed in sentiments and just feel like pouring them down on paper. No doubt there is some beauty in such expressions, too.

In this book, I've expressed my thoughts on some of the issues that troubled me at a young age. Those issues have given birth to ideas, and we all know that an idea comes with a form—a natural, novel form. I have tried to express those ideas or themes with precision, flow, and in a suitable tone. To what extent I've been successful, only you'll decide. I hope this collection is worth your time and attention.

With Love,

Vikas.

1. My Conflicts and Conclusions

I was down and despairing,

Many things I was missing;

Soon became grateful to God,

As I started counting my blessings!

I was bothered by judgements,

And took seriously public opinion;

Realised I'm accountable only to God,

Not to the whims and fancies of clods.

I was gathering fragments of a broken heart,

And thought love to be a deceptive craft,

Then I realised my mistakes continual,

I went for beauty and overlooked principles.

Status comes by meeting social expectations,

That's why happiness is a rare occasion;

Eventually stopped caring for such limitations,

And started following my heart's inclinations.

I was losing poise to chase my ambitions,

As I lacked skill and cosy situations;

Now I think delay will impart maturity,

Sharpen observation and refine sense of beauty!

2. Commerce

Life is a trade-off,

Commerce is the rule of the game.

I wanted skill,

Currency was hard work;

I desired maturity,

Now the price was pain;

I want happiness presently,

Coins are now contentment.

I want to decode love,

The keys are heartbreak and heartburn;

To assess one's family's love,

The prerequisite is social failure:

If we want to know our true friends,

The price, we all know, is difficult times;

If we desire social status,

We've to succumb to social expectations.

If we want acceptance from all,

The demand is servile submission;

For mental peace,

We've to choose the undesirable solitude;

For abundance of money,

There is necessity of being ethically neutral;

If we want company,

We've to sacrifice our individuality.

For all our desires,

The price is predecided;

Life seems to be continual commerce,

For a blessing to be credited,

Something is always debited;

The creation seems to be perfectly symmetrical,

All exchanges precisely mathematical,

For every smile, there is a debt to pay,

And we dance to the tunes of commerce, almost every day!

3. Confessions of a Salesman

First day of the job after MBA completion,

Assistant Manager Marketing & Sales, was the designation;

With a heart beating fast, entered company's sales office,

We've to sell flats, was instantly brought to my notice:

Absolutely no idea, about the corporate culture,

Equally ignorant of the sales profession and its true nature.

Boss was not impressed by me, in the first meeting,

As he was a talkative, boyish kind, unlike me;

Four flats target, as expectations next to nil,

First sales call, luckily two successful deals!

Next month's target increased to eight,

Target overachieved, sold twenty-three flats straight:

The strategy was, "Sell yourself first!"

Dress, courtesy, communication and pitch,

Patience, common sense and the personality switch!

Always in formals, and a tie with loose knot,

Tightening it before meetings, in weather humid and hot;

Quickly judging the customers, calm despite stress,

Never lost the case, when chose to impress:

Aggressive selling instincts, reached its zenith,

Hapless morality, pushed to the back seat;

If you've money, you've to purchase,

Wolves of real estate, are on the chase.

Professional demeanour, outwardly sedate,

From within, a devil incarnates!

Skills of humour, a bit of wiles,

When everything failed, just a parting smile.

Rich businessmen, elegant ladies,

Sharp CEOs, middle-class families:

Bandra to Virar, Andheri to Cuff Parade,

Enjoying the evenings, mastering the trade;

Dining and partying, with colleagues and the boss,

Reading and writing went for a toss;

Corporate life's secrets quickly decoded,

Bombay scanned; competitors decimated.

Very soon realised, the product is overpriced,

And we've been hired to trick and beguile;

Loyal to the company, but am I just to the customers?

This disturbing question, emerged at regular intervals;

Ethical conflicts, tortured every day,

Life-costing conscience caused dismay;

One fine morning, resigned from the job,

Adieu glitter, back to the roads.

Now I'm selling, knowledge and insights,

Clients are my pupils, jolly and bright;

But I must confess, there is twist in the tale,

Once in sales, always in sales!

4. Modern Youth

Oh God, today's modern youths!

Quite often, I hear this disillusioned remark;

An opinion lacking positive sentiments...

All my students belong to this category,

Naturally, I cannot ignore this perception conveniently;

So, today I'm in the college, purposely with a critical eye,

Leaving aside my academic concerns for a while.

Bright boys and sharp girls,

Freely chatting, oblivious of the world;

Energy and excitement all around,

Whether inside the classroom or on the ground;

Some girls reticent, others talkative,

Some boys flamboyant, others circumspective;

Spontaneity and wit, candid confidence,

Refined manners, fine aesthetic sense;

Chosen few, academically bright,

Some even possess, intellectual might!

Free from complexes, hardly knowing prejudices,

A gust of fresh breeze, amid stale premises;

Variety and uniqueness, multifarious personalities,

Delightful samples, of God's creativity!

Naturally, I was forced to think of the seniors too,

It's dreadful to share, my conclusions true!

Frequently opinionated, and quite judgemental;

Craft perennial, double standards perpetual;

Majority of us, facing mid-life crisis,

In life's blistering desert, searching for an oasis.

Meaningless debates, suffocating conversations,

Uncouth tempers, behind the veneer of sophistication;

The picture seems a bit, dull and dismal,

No doubt there are, exceptions occasional.

It's true youths are moody, with some lifestyle aberrations,

And their frivolity, requires urgent rectifications;

Still, I would like, to safely believe,

That this generation, is quite a relief.

Of myriad endowments, shades and persona,

One day they'll become, individuals with charisma;

Gleeful adolescents, jaunty in their heydays,

May they blossom beautifully, and bloom without delay!

5. Nothing like...

Nothing like an intimate friend,

A relief in stress,

A rock in distress;

Nothing like a good book,

Stirring us to defy, the pervading servitude,

A perpetual joy, a bliss in solitude.

Nothing like a diligent artist,

Striving incessantly for perfection,

To give ecstatic thrill, to many generations;

Nothing like a sprightly, pretty woman,

With an appeal, to the man inside us,

An inspiration for suavity, affluence and status.

Nothing like an overcast sky,

Moonlit evenings and starry nights,

Like the fragrant flowers, colourful and bright;

Nothing like the frank, young boys,

Their nonchalant laughter, humour dark,

And indeed, their witty remarks!

Nothing like girls' modesty,

Their giggles and blush, voice and smile,

And their calculated, artful guise;

Nothing like a youthful old man,

His happy acceptance of age,

Sharing priceless wisdom and enlightening messages.

Nothing like intellectual subtleties,

Productive reflections for perceptual clarity,

A technique to decode, life's baffling perplexities.

The list is endless,

God's mercy, is truly limitless,

Life is not, as appalling as it appears,

There is always a hope, for smile in tears.

6. Road to Modernity

First day in the Hindu College, after migrating from Ramjas;

Felt out of place, a fish out of water;

Hindu was a happening college then!

Sophisticated boys, elegant girls,

Chirping birds, shining like pearls.

Lovely, graceful Ma'ams, and the popular spots,

Mecca, Tarana and the library, Jai Singh lawn and what not!

But I used to repent my decision to migrate,

Alone most of the time, silent and sedate;

Classmates neither cold, nor welcoming,

Waiting to test my merit, before befriending.

Affectionate teachers, the only saving grace,

Still, many complications, I had to face:

Quickly realised, my defects in personality,

Boys' school conditioning, was costing me dearly;

I used to struggle, while conversing with girls,

Not knowing how to dress up, and a bit temperamental;

But I must confess, I accepted the challenge,

Come what may, I'll cover the entire range.

Dress and thoughts, the art of communication,

Impressing pretty damsels, was the sinister intention;

Tact and decency, a little bit of humour,

No serious talks, or grave demeanour;

Carefully scanning, the nature of madame,

Adjusting accordingly, with wit and elan;

Some may call it trick, or guile you might say,

This is the price my dearest, to be amiable we pay.

Deep down sensitive, outwardly cool,

Personality switch, was the path to the moons;

There is hardly any victory, or concrete tangible gain,

Yet I have had, my share in the game;

As a friend I seldom lacked, but was foolishly romantic,

Very late realised, my ways unrealistic.

Soul, mind, heart and some sense of beauty,

Are of cosmetic relevance, if not without utility:

Just growing as a man and refining perceptions,

I know not why it is, my priority and conviction;

Still, I must say, there is a sense of achievement,

For a small city boy, ordinary and ignorant;

It's true I'm disillusioned with many aspects of life,

Sometimes I wish I had, a daughter and a loving wife!

7. Valentine - A Wish

Love is not love if it obeys reason,

Not if it changes with seasons;

Not at all if it searches for options,

And easily accepts separation.

Love was when she nervously blushed,

And walked with downcast eyes;

Her cheeks with excitement flushed,

When I looked into her beautiful eyes.

Heaven, what an evening it was,

When I touched her hands, soft and warm,

An intoxicating fragrance she had worn,

With a dazzling smile to disarm;

That night I was actually in a trance,

O, her breath, her dress and her glance!

Quite often, our eyes later met,

A hope for a possible romance;

Her tender, husky voice always struck,

Like a sharp-edged weapon or a lance;

My heart always skipped a beat,

When close to me, she took a seat;

Her cheeks with excitement flushed,

When I looked into her beautiful eyes.

What's our life, after all,

In the absence of love and romance?

Nothing but a dull, monotonous obligation,

Besides being a slave of chance.

We all fall in love at least once,

Despite our wisdom or logic;

Go for chemistry, I beseech ye,

You'll soon see its beauty and magic!

8. The Colors of Life

Success, we know, is a long battle,

Happiness, a mirage or a theme subtle,

Status, largely a fool's paradise,

Road to contentment has many hurdles.

Yet I think it's a lovely world,

Beauty everywhere, explicit or covert;

God's blessings are actually infinite,

And His creation is really fantastic.

A daughter's love for her doting father,

And sons' latent commitment to their mothers;

Childhood ecstasies, romantic delights,

Friendly leg-pulling and playful fights.

Birds' twitter, cute toddlers,

A courteous kid, pets and flowers;

A teenage girl, anxious for attention,

Boys' quick scan with silent admiration:

Brother's silence after sister's marriage,

A friend's support, an encouraging message.

Genuine eyes, unaffected style,

A blush of modesty with a sweet smile;

A warm lady with girlish charm,

Elderly gentlemen with grace and elan.

A disciplinarian mother, principled father,

Forgiving siblings, unconditional lovers;

A brilliant playwright, a precise thinker,

A master lyricist, a world-class scholar.

Loyal partners, teasing romance,

Sincere compliments, a disarming glance;

Magnificent nature, moon and fountains,

Green dark forests, brooks and mountains;

Rivers and oceans, cool evening breeze,

Rainbow and drizzle, long night's ease.

The world is beauteous, so is the journey,

A job as per liking, little bit of money;

Doing our duty in peace or strife,

Let's enjoy the delightful colors of life!

9. Our English Class

Mr Singh calmly waited for his students to come,

In our school, the teacher's room was fixed, and students used to move;

Sometimes we were 'in time', sometimes 'on time',

Then he would ask me to take attendance;

With a certain pride, I used to do the needful!

And now the class begins.

Paragraphs of a poem or prose would be read by the pupils,

And Mr Singh then would explain the meaning;

Sources of stories would be told,

Further meaning and context of difficult words would be discussed;

Sometimes Emily Bronte's 'Heathcliff' would torment 'Catherine',

Next day Mr Wordsworth would wander lonely as a cloud;

On some occasions, H W Longfellow would philosophise about life,

And then Robert Frost would remember the promises he had to keep,

But please don't forget Miss Eliot's 'Silas Marner' in this august company!

'Serious students' would note down every word spoken by their esteemed teacher,

Happily, I was one of them in those days!

And those days were exceptions to my otherwise lackadaisical academic life;

O studies, forgive my base inconstancy!

Then Mr Singh would write pronunciation in IPA and discuss phonetics,

Bewildered and amused, we would look at each other and communicate through eyes;

What a bliss it was to listen to Mr R N Singh's lectures!

Oh, how badly I miss those beautiful days!

But life being what it is,

now I find myself in the same role;

But I know I'm a poor match to Mr R N Singh's standard,

After all, one cannot match perfection;

And he was handsome, I must tell you,

Gracefully stylish too!

O Shelley, how right thou art!

'Style is the man' literally as well as metaphorically:

A unique blend of looks, knowledge and skill,

Numerous memories linger still:

Once the classes finished, I'd go back to my hostel,

Religiously peruse the notes at leisure;

Collect the words of my choosing and revise at intervals,

Even try to frame my own sentences.

Sometimes we would study simplified Shakespeare,

And would refuse to consider him a great writer,

As commonplace his plots used to appear,

Only now I realise Shakespeare's brilliance,

It is all about characterisation and thematic excellence!

Mr R N Singh, his charisma and the English Class,

Will remain precious to me till the very last;

My life has not been easy,

But I am rarely sad;

God has mercifully blessed me with some priceless blessings,

Which I'm unwilling to exchange for a comfortable destiny.

If I'm given a chance to choose my life again,

I want the same struggles and the very same pain;

You may alter everything else if such is your intention,

But please give me the same teachers and the very same education!

10. An Evening to Remember

It was a boring, calm evening,

In a small cafeteria, with a cup of tea, I was sitting;

Alone, quite alone.

Lost in my own world and thoughts,

In that mood when we're neither happy nor distraught.

There was no one in the cafe except two girls,

Equally engrossed in their affairs and talk;

The one facing me was of nice, soothing appearance:

But sometimes, we intend to look beyond outward beauty;

Might be in her late twenties or early thirties,

Feminine charm and captivating simplicity.

These days I try to read eyes and smile too,

As everything else is just God's gift, and I think it's true!

So, I started analysing her apparatus of sight,

Clear, gentle, sensitive eyes;

Stealthily, I gave her intermittent glances with feigned indifference;

Mademoiselle was sharp enough to take note of it;

In fact, all dames are sharp in this regard!

Then there was a smile on her face;

It had a sad texture, yet it was pleasing;

A bit of appearance, some personality and a natural constitution,

Appeal to men of all generations;

On this ever-enchanting topic, I wanted to continue my reflections,

But the confounded tea was exhausted!

Unwillingly I came out of the place with grave expression,

I know not how I became aware of my unceasing trials and other complications.

So, I was out, again amid the tumultuous crowd;

Brooding upon the past and the uncertain future;

Yet the breeze and surroundings seemed pleasing to me,

And the images of the cafe kept flashing;

I was still lost in my world and musings,

But the evening was no longer calm, no longer boring!

11. Teacher's Day

It's Teacher's Day today,

A day to express our gratitude to the teachers,

Who made us sensible creatures;

Some of them had profound knowledge,

Others were warm and had an emotional edge.

Committed to a cause, alike in comfort or in climes wuthering,

Godsent angels to those who claim just a few blessings;

Quite often, our achievements only decide our worth in society,

And people are quick to judge us at the first opportunity;

But our teachers show faith in our abilities,

When the world is disillusioned with us or doubts our utility.

When we're young, the teachers give us intellectual light,

Their lectures, sometimes, are sheer delight;

Majorly it's our teachers who shape our personality,

And instil within us a sense of propriety;

They demolish our delusions and clear our perceptions,

Domesticate our passions and sharpen our imagination.

• 28 •

We may not always be glittering achievers,

Still, we get love from our generous teachers;

Maybe these divine souls are eternal part of our destiny,

Or maybe with these gentlemen, we have deep-rooted chemistry!

12. Love-I

First it was a pretty face,

Then a dancing shape;

Later, perhaps, lovely eyes,

Further gleaming hair and appealing voice;

Frivolous nature kept on changing the definition of beauty,

But the heart searched for precise answers and clarity;

Experience proved futile, everything mentioned above,

As time passed by, my perceptions changed as regards
Love.

Fell for girls once or twice on above qualifications,

Obviously, nothing came out of it, barring heartburn and
palpitations!

Maybe the parameters were weak and shaky,

What still haunted was the same question, baffling and
tricky!

Who is, after all, a beauty worth falling for?

Which kind of romance is free from injury or embarrassing
torpor?

Diligent observations followed and a bit of reflection too,

Ah me! It was smile I missed regarding this mysterious issue!

Smile! Almost always revealing the secrets of heart and soul!

A functional conscience making a loving persona on the whole!

A thinking mind adding permanence to initial attraction,

Establishing an ever-blooming chemistry and ever-increasing passion;

A tolerable appearance, I realise, is enough for a mate;

But alas! Such a valuable realisation, and so late!

O ignorance, thy blissful presence in youth and stings in later years!

Yet better late than never, as they say, my dear!

The time is ticking away and it waits for none,

Life seems to slip away and the past can't be undone;

Yet there is no urgency or a hurry,

I'm still hoping for a tryst, leaving aside all worries;

A lady, someday, may think of me with romantic fervour,

And Love might dawn with all its fragrance and splendour!

13. Self-motivation

What life is, I could never know for sure,

Conclusions change with time,

Sometimes even with mood,

Long years of enquiry, yet there is no clarity.

Though everyone around seems happy,

Still, I guess it's a common dilemma,

Approaches to life are just opinions, a matter of
definitions,

Local relevance only, not universality.

Getting a job, raising kids, and spending time,

A popular definition of life,

It's a solution or escape,

I don't know;

Some take refuge in imagination,

Expression of some noble sentiments,

Some utopian ideas or fanciful dreams,

These talks hardly appeal to me, charming balderdash.

Devising new schemes every day,

To make life interesting is not easy,

Presently, a new technique appeals to me,

One day at a time!

A sleep of six-seven hours,

Some study, a bit of reflection,

Writing, if possible, efforts for new learnings,

Work for the livelihood,

Trying to do justice to the pennies received,

A bit of humour, little bit of recreation,

Forgetting past, and no fancy plans for future.

So, just living for today,

Accepting God's design for the day,

Assessment at night, while going to sleep,

Of the positives, negatives, fortunes or misfortunes.

Finally, the present only,

Nothing to do with the past or future,

Just living in the moments,

Making the best out of it,

Accepting and enjoying my lot,

Meek submission to the will of Almighty God!

14. The Comprehension

A book is known by its conceptual clarity,

A poem, by emotional honesty;

A student is known by his academic sincerity,

A teacher, by affectionate commitment;

Parents are known by the manners of their kids,

Individuals, by self-belief.

A play is known by its characterisation,

A novel, by an engaging plot;

Humanities is insightful observation,

Science, a matter of approach;

Music is known by its appeal to heart,

A movie, should appeal to intellect.

A woman is known by the choice of her partner,

A man, by his principles;

Charm lies in naturalness,

Depth, in discretion;

Poise is to domesticate passion,

Sprightliness, love for life!

Growth lies in reflection,

Improvement, in introspection;

Skill requires untiring perseverance,

Creativity, a free spirit;

Artistic excellence lies in purpose,

Business, is justice to the customers.

God has made a lovely world,

And He is the only player!

We are all just puppets,

Dancing to the tunes of Almighty God.

Our reactions to the circumstances, define us,

Cynicism is negative response to harsh truths,

Acknowledging ground realities is not being a pessimist,

We can always be cautiously optimistic!

Beauty, after all, is the foundation of creation,

Let the heart remain functional,

And mind continues to be analytical!

15. Life

What life is, I often reflect,

Definitive answer, I never get;

What's within reach, where we're helpless,

Difficult it is, to precisely assess;

Though not sure, but a tentative understanding,

Often comes, after pragmatic musings.

Life is an exciting quest,

With curiosity and intellect!

It's status and having an ambition,

Getting affluence and admiration!

It's sensitivity and conscience,

Benevolence and excellence;

Will-power and manhood,

Demarcate its altitude!

No doubt there are trials,

And heartbreaking denials;

These are destiny's trick to educate,

Almighty's design which we call fate;

Hence enjoy the journey, for achievements do not wait,

Just love and laugh, let the joy mutate!

16. Netarhat School

We all love our alma mater,

Where our being is shaped and we learn academic rigour;

Teachers, they are our role model,

To educate, discipline, love and counsel;

What is Netarhat we could never understand,

Just a school, a concept, an idea or a wonderland!

We Hatians love our childhood mainly because of
Netarhat,

Time spent there is etched on the deepest recesses of heart;

Tournaments, collective feasting, antyakshari, athletics and
dramatics,

Art, music, science, language, humanities and mathematics;

And the Final Exam! Heartbeat increasing with every
passing moment,

Mistake of one mark was enough to increase discontent.

Visiting Haat secretly with friends without permission,

Sojourn in Lower Ghaghri was pleasant digressions;

Mataji's warmth and hospitality in Holi,

Cold days sometimes and nights often chilly;

Our teachers taught us independence of thought,

To have an opinion and never give up before having fought;

We are a blend of modern outlook with roots in tradition,

Flowers of the same garden, of different fragrances and variations.

We are Doctors, Engineers, Bureaucrats and in Teaching,

Managers, Lawyers, CAs and in Shipping;

Wherever we are, we leave our mark,

Try not to let our teachers down and make a difference stark;

Affectionate juniors, lovely friends and wonderful seniors,

Source of motivation, learning and humour;

May this light of education keep on illuminating us,

And make our life eventful, fulfilling and blissfully joyous!

17. Mr K N Vasudevan

Scholarly gait, elegant style;

Brilliance personified, academic smile;

Modern outlook, vision smart;

Affectionate to pupils, simplicity of heart;

A man of principles, probity and dignity;

Epitomising wit, skill and versatility;

Warm to colleagues, helpful to friends;

Sensible and sensitive, aware of latest trends.

An administrator and a leader with finesse;

A man lively and of angelic grace;

Often when I brood over my fortune and blessings,

Teachers like KNV always flash upon my mind;

A passionate longing is simply I am left with,

May God always let loose academicians of his kind!

18. My Soulmate

I have a soulmate,

Yes, I think I have,

She is calm and a bit melancholy,

Upon my heart, her monopoly,

Yet a girl lovely and sedate,

A beauty of first-rate,

She is not mine,

Yet her soul is mine.

Sweet, fair and appealing,

And fair in her dealings;

Her cheek is normally flushed,

Whenever there is a blush,

Undoubtedly, my strongest crush.

A bit harsh to me,

But to the world, she is a Sweetie;

Not my possession in this birth,

But is in my heart everywhere on earth.

I just have to say to her,

That someday there won't be any obstructions,

I'm waiting for death to remove restrictions,

Then we'd fly in the air,

In each other arms, always together.

19. Tryst Futile

A broken heart's pang,

Sometimes difficult to tolerate,

Seeking refuge in the comforting smoke,

Smoke mingling with the dull surroundings,

Blood boiling after the violence,

Education mitigating anger,

But the heart is still disturbed,

The mind still tortured.

Society bewildered, not knowing where to go,

The ruffians have taken the responsibility,

I know not with what agenda,

Smoke mixing with the beats of heart,

Many beings melting within me.

Pain cutting deeper and deeper,

The heart is almost dead,

Only bones and mind are left,

And a functional conscience,

Sometimes sentiments tell me,

Now let us call it a day,

But there is a call of duty,

Which is not easy to ignore.

Mind reflecting in the stillness of the air,

Seeking ease in days gone by,

Lost in vacant musings,

But there is a glimmer of light,

Some kids here and there with watchful eyes,

Waiting for the opportunity of service,

Sacrificing everything for society and nation,

And then my spirit revitalises,

And once again optimism captivates me,

And once again I set my eyes on the stars,

And join the struggles of life!

20. The Crush...

Perhaps the only thing worth remembering in my life,

My Crushes, my lovely sweethearts!

Yes, they loved me,

There is no pain involved, Mutuality of emotions,

Romantic acceptance as a man,

No negativity, just love,

Admiration, attention and kindness,

No man in this world can possibly face this,

Without being floored,

Disarmed, charmed, won.

Majorly my classmates, some neighbours too,

One Ma'am, MBA, same age,

Please forgive me, I still respect her,

Yet sometimes, logic fails.

Used to teach us Brand Management,

Never asked any question to me,

In fact, never ever looked at me!

Actually, she had a difficult time teaching me.

I was a bit mischievous with the MBA Ma'am,

Never missed the opportunity to admire her on campus,

And she knew it,

A woman in totality, an intelligent elegant lady.

Some girls were quite junior to me,

There was always a sense of loss,

I was either ahead or behind,

Never at the right place, at the right time,

But love being love,

There was never a desire to possess,

Quick to realise they are not in my destiny,

Just a feel-good factor, a sweet memory,

And I was always happy with this.

First one, my classmate in boarding school,

She used to stay in staff quarters, her mother being a nurse in the hospital,

Always had some excuse to hover around her home,

Never talked though,

Once went to her place to invite her mom to some
function,

Fortunately, she only came out to receive me,

Said whatever I could somehow say,

She just nodded and smiled, she knew well my intentions,

All girls, however decent, are experts in these matters,

You can't befool them, what's the need after all.

Then another, when I was in 12th, hostel,

She was in girls' hostel,

Many girls in the hostel somehow knew me,

Helped them a lot in the final exams,

Obviously unethically, yet no regret, lovely girls!

I think she loved me genuinely,

But I was fool enough not to understand it,

When I was coming to Delhi for graduation,

She just said, "You'll meet pretty girls there, I guess."

Forgive me, love, maybe next birth.

Then this girl, possibly the most beautiful girl in the
college then,

She had a boyfriend,

I was a good boy then, still I'm, as per my assessment,

She knew my moral dilemma,

Took some subtle initiatives,

But as I said, I was a good boy!

On farewell day, I wrote a poem on her,

Tears trickled down her cheeks, just said,

"You are going to be a good poet."

I hope I've not let her down,

Lovely girl!

Then a young girl of the colony, when I was a UPSC aspirant,

Every evening, she would wait for me,

I was regular with my evening walks,

Maybe for this particular reason, not health,

One would be very nervous when crossing my way,

Once almost fell, she was in heels,

And then once, hit a stone while walking,

Ignoring all social norms,

I asked, "Are you okay?"

Then said," While walking, we need to be attentive."

In an elder brotherly tone.

I'd often complain to God for sending me a bit early on earth,

Then she was married, and I was still preparing for UPSC,

She always had very sweet feelings for me, never disrespectful,

Ever grateful little heart,

May God give you every possible happiness!

Then there was a classmate in MBA,

I've never seen a mature girl so natural,

I would openly give her compliments,

And she'd take it sportingly,

A beauty in totality.

One recent case too,

Seems a very old connection,

Three decades old.

One of many young flowers,

But someone related since teens,

Let's not discuss it now,

I'm waiting for time's verdict,

Though once you cross death,

Time loses relevance,

Seems like my soulmate,

Feel her presence every moment,

In my heart, in my mind too,

Maybe 'paradise regained' for me.

So sometimes early, sometimes late,

By and large, it has been my fate,

Death perhaps will give me a chance,

Hence, I've decided to patiently wait!

21. The Last Love...

A man busy with his work,

A lecture is going on,

A kind of premonition surging within,

Yet will-power summoned,

Somehow striking a balance between studies and
sentiments.

Feigned ignorance from both sides,

A lovely lady flashing frequently,

Beautiful girl in beautiful attire,

The man trying to focus on duty,

Still a bit of heartbeat.

Some calling, some familiar callings,

Of what moment I cannot say with definiteness,

Yet some relation, maybe past beckoning to the heart,

A divine impulse or some calculation?

Love or a passing whim?

Something pure or flimsy?

Maybe none of these,

Maybe a genuine, tender sentiment,

Let's wait for the test of time.

One fine morning, peculiar sensations,

As if somebody pulling me with ferocity!

Reason I know not,

But the intensity I could feel,

Somebody entering within me,

Maybe a soulmate,

Yet no clarity,

Blood mixing with the complementary tonality.

Then clarity, one fine morning,

Non-duality experienced,

Yes, a soulmate!

The meeting place again,

Heartbeat increasing without any reason,

A girl with a boy,

Downcast eye, scared and apologetic,

Ah me, a love triangle again!

Heartbroken…

Still, I'd opine, there are some battles of life in which,

Losing is a better option,

Romantic keep?

Yes, but it's the lesser evil,

Sometimes we've to choose between lesser evils,

God has been kind to me,

I can say this with a bit of surety.

But do I deserve this always in the name of love?

No answer...

Maybe my destiny, but the decision taken,

No such buffoonery again,

Let it be the last love.

Whether Love's labour lost or not,

Is now irrelevant,

No further romantic adventure,

Let the story terminate here only,

The last love or lost love losing all relevance,

Simply waiting to see whether we are related or not.

• 55 •

22. Post-mortem of Love

I'm a non-believer in romantic love,

Not in its occurrence but in its completion,

Marriage, here, has always been a social relation,

Hence complications, myriad calculations…

That's why passion, however intense, ultimately dies a natural death,

And both the parties enjoy life as if nothing ever happened;

That's the beauty of life,

Change is the only constant!

Constant in flux is just a sweet illusion…

Twice I was seriously in love,

For want of better term, let's call it love.

On both occasions entangled in the familiar 'Love Triangle'

O 'LT', thou art more fatal than the Bermuda Triangle!

What a gem in destiny's multiplicities of trials!

If you don't understand metaphysics, you are considered a kid in philosophy,

Likewise, if you've missed, ' Love triangle ',

You're a baby in the 'games of romance'

I claim some kind of expertise in this bumpy terrain,

If not a mature doctorate;

Ah me, what a torturous experience!

What an emotional perdition and an intellectual puzzle!

If you consider physics and chemistry difficult,

You are, probably, innocent,

You can clear all concepts of science in ten months,

But even ten years is insufficient for precise analysis of such
a 'triangle'!

Damsels of my time had no ordinary skills in such sports,

Some of them deserve 'gold medals' in this game!

Now gracefully retired,

Obviously, once you reach Mount Everest,

You don't feel like sitting there the rest of your life.

By God's grace, I always had romantic advantages in such
triangles,

With social advantages, God chose to bless my rivals,

Obviously, God is just and knows no partiality,

I've never met a guy who, surprisingly, has both
advantages!

And the lady in the centre, somehow, would desire best of
both worlds,

Hence the conception of the famous, ' Love triangles',

A marvel of creativity of a few brilliant feminine minds!

So, one boy would get the heart, another loyalty of mind,

And decision is, normally, taken by mind.

But not an easy decision,

Heart wants fulfilment, appetite creating conflicts,

Destiny not being kind to provide both,

It was a frequent case in my days, two decades back,

Obviously, sad overall, for ladies too,

Girls are, actually, accountable to family, friends and
relatives,

They couldn't destroy their world for just one individual,

"After all, husbands are also caring,"

One of my muses once told me,

And the mouse replied, "One-year care of a husband can't
match the love of a lover for a day,"

Heavy dialogue, but of no avail,

My soulmate always knew that she was incapable of countering her lover's logic,

But both the sweethearts followed their reasons,

Romance has always been a poor match to 'Finance',

But wait, things are not as simple as it appears,

Both the queens at last agreed to offer conjugal bliss,

Ultimately heart prevailed!

But the boy politely declined,

As he thought very soon familiarity would breed contempt,

Heart can survive without fulfilment,

Materiality can't be ignored for long,

My conclusion, in fact, conviction, is, if a boy is not accepted within a week,

He'll never be wholeheartedly accepted.

Sometimes I feel, a man-woman relation is not only about instincts,

The non-physical aspects also matter,

Maybe the values, attitude, manners, aesthetics or simply the gaze,

Maybe just eyes, or smile or sometimes voice,

In some cases, as trivial as modesty becomes the primary concern,

You never know what will make a person appealing, lovable, a potential partner,

But essentially, it's the society which calls the shot, unlike West.

Initially, there was bitterness,

Now I'm reconciled to it, maybe we were not compatible,

Maybe it was not settled in heaven.

It was not their fault, I guess,

It was just a matter of priority,

Perhaps social advantage is the real blessing.

Hopefully, they are happy now,

Maybe a day/a year claim was not valid.

In the times of social media,

You know what's happening in your friend's life,

They seem to enjoy life, a complete family life,

Yet, somewhere there is something missing,

They are still pretty, but the shine is gone,

They are still appealing, but the sharp edge is no longer there,

Their smile is still pleasing but the soul is gone.

Sometimes it's not easy to accept a person,

Yet sometimes, it's not easy to ignore the old flame, after rejection!

23. A Broken Heart

It's a beautiful world,

But a sad world,

Quite often I sense the pangs of rejection,

A bruised manhood, a violated womanhood,

I had similar experiences when I was young,

Really a traumatic experience, scary, hellish,

Here are my conclusions.

Rejection in a romantic relationship is very demoralising,

It creates doubt about our self-worth,

It shakes our foundations,

Questions raised to our existence,

One person's opinion, and so devastating!

Initially, there is intense negativity,

Violence of many kinds follows, verbal, emotional, psychological,

Base attacks, display of brute instincts,

Actually, it's a defence mechanism,

Offence is the best defence!

But not needed, not expected from a decent person,

I feel the relationship is tested when it ends,

Yes, the colour of dissolving bond,

Let's respect the relation we once had,

At least there were some good moments,

There is no point in grievances,

We can't force someone to love us,

Same principles apply to respect, loyalty, and other good things,

Let's communicate the tears through silence, loud, graceful silence,

No childish tantrums.

We are not meant to be together, that's it,

Compatibility missing,

He has not rejected me,

He has rejected the alliance, the possible togetherness,

He was not comfortable with the relationship,

Not a fulfilling one, as per his expectations,

I could not qualify as per some of his parameters,

As many boys don't qualify mine,

Someone else might find me suitable.

A rich boy, my friend, was rejected for lack of
qualifications,

A qualified boy was not accepted due to lack of money,
quite frequently,

Both can't be worthless at the same time,

Just a matter of priorities, nothing serious,

Sometimes a boy, rich as well as qualified, is rejected for
personality,

Occasionally for appearance,

Quite often for lack of sense of humour.

Men and women are on equal footing on this issue,

In fact, but for physicality, men and women are perfectly
equal,

Beauty, appeal, intelligence, manners, anything can be a
possible reason for non-acceptance.

Finally understood one thing,

She didn't love me, he didn't love you,

They didn't value us, so simple,

Why is it beside the point, irrelevant, inconsequential,

There was no love actually,

Otherwise, she would have stayed with me, he with you,

Period.

There is no point in researching the reason for dislike,

Can be a trivial reason,

I loved him, he lost commitment,

He didn't love me, I lost nothing,

Good that I know now the reality,

I was living in an imaginary world,

As simple as that.

Quite often, the reason for heartbreak,

Is the wrong assessment of the person,

He is good to me; how does it matter if he is not nice to others,

No dear, it's gross misjudgement,

No individual can carry contradictory value system,

Let the opportunity come; he'll show his true colours,

It's just an opportunistic alliance presently,

Fault lies with you, not him,

There is no point in complaining now,

In future, judge a person by his behaviour with strangers,

Still, in the final analysis,

You'll get the partner you deserve, don't worry at all.

I have had a detailed study,

Trust me, God makes matches as per our worth,

Appearance, personality, values, qualification and status,

Nature can be complimentary;

I'm yet to find an exception to this rule,

So final opinion!

Sooner or later, you'll come to the same conclusions.

Now still there is anxiety, restlessness, possessiveness,

And this is love, you may believe so,

No, it's not love; it's our ego,

We are not troubled with love, actually,

We are not troubled by the loss of an individual,

But the loss of self-esteem,

I had very high opinion of myself,

Now the truth is staring at me,

We are actually worried about ourselves, not the person
who left us,

Otherwise, also he was not extraordinary,

We know it.

I thought I'm charming, But I was mistaken,

For her, success had real charm,

She might be lenient to her brother, her friend,

But to the man of her life, never.

He has to be someone she can be proud of,

As she'll be identified with him socially,

And she should also be a matter of pride to him,

To flaunt her in his circles, him in her society,

Quite justified.

You may complain, then why did she take initiative,

Relevant question,

Maybe you were approved by her instincts, maybe by her
heart,

Maybe a sense if aesthetics,

But dear, you are not appealing enough to her social
instincts,

So just let it be.

If an individual blames the family for failure of
relationship,

He is looking for an excuse,

Simply he didn't love you,

Likewise, she, too, was not serious,

She was not in love when the story began,

All confessions regarding gradual development of love,

Is a fool's paradise,

If there is no love initially,

It'll never be there.

So just cheer up, improve your worth,

Let there be no doubt regarding this,

If a girl is proud of your love,

Only God can prevent her from being yours,

No papa, no mummy,

No third-party responsibility.

Same rule applies to boys,

So, girls and boys, don't worry, someone special is waiting
for you,

Just stay away from chocolates and ice-creams and dinner,
brief and early,

I'm 47, single, still hopeful,

Then why are you sad in your teens?

Just take heart, enjoy and smile.

24. Beauty, thy name is Woman!

The first category is the 'Romantics',

Sweetest of all, every boy's dream,

They generally have a good face,

They're always dressed well, mostly gracefully,

Nice colour combinations,

A bit reticent, shy and feminine,

They don't believe in male friends,

Out and out romantic, that's why,

They are courteous to boys,

Will never indulge in loose talks,

Know the limits,

Lover of music, soft songs generally,

They don't trust men easily,

But if, by chance, they like you,

They will marry you, will fight for you, convince their father,

One-man women will have respect for social norms,

Loyal, committed, decent,

Even when they are old,

They possess the girlish charms,

Vitality and vigour of spirit,

But alas, they are few and far between!

And then there are 'Style icons',

An absolute beauty, some sort of bliss, poetry material!

Love personified!

Sharp, sensitive, mature, modern,

In one word, 'Elegant',

These beauties are true delights,

Fine companions, lovely partners, queens on all fronts,

They know men, they value men,

They know that money is a poor match to personality,

Your knowledge and intelligence are relevant only for this category,

Someday, God willing...

Then there are 'Liberals',

Appealing, attractive, sometimes pretty too,

The best of the lot, God sent angels,

Unlike the popular notion, I always find them genuine,
sober, tender,

Non-believer in tantalising,

No apology for a good physique,

Nothing to do with the norms! yes ma'am,

We approve; we admire; we salute your spirit.

These women are genuinely interested in boys,

Natural, bold, no hypocrisy,

They take pride in their womanhood,

No crisis, no complexes, no doubts,

I'm pretty, and I have some 'appeal',

And thanks for your attention,

Yes, they are always grateful!

But to be handled delicately,

A bit mature, modern outlook required,

No judgement, please.

Then there are the 'boy-lovers', a passionate kind, a bit
moody,

Girls with childish temperaments,

They don't have even a single female friend,

I know this category very closely, sadly,

One of my sweethearts was such a girl,

Obviously, the same gender is not lenient to your idiocies,
hence no friend,

These girls are interesting species,

They know your name, still they'll ask,

They know your number, birthday etc., still they'll ask,

They don't want to show interest actually,

Deliberately reply late, will try to make you possessive,
using her friends,

But what's the need dear, I'm already yours!

Maybe they want to increase the intensity,

Maybe they are stupid enough not to know what to do,

They love you, but won't accept it, hardly ever express,

Scared of being decoded,

But I know you're sensitive, not sure about your
compatibility,

Maybe you doubt your abilities as a companion,

And that's why feel confident only with the nincompoops,

Your assumed gravity, a defence mechanism, is of no use my love,

Your expressions say everything, your heart written on your face,

Just be natural, genuine, normal, please...

One best friend, obviously a moron, 2-3 close friends, rest friends,

And she'd discuss intimate things with them in the name of 'modernity',

I'm happy being regressive God,

Please don't make me such a 'Modern' man ever,

And she has a romantic interest too!

Whom she'll deliberately ignore,

She'd dress up too, God knows for whom,

Always in denial mode,

It hurts her ego to be obvious, yes, self-respect she hardly knows,

So, one step ahead, two steps back next day,

Normally these girls suffer from doubts,

Appearance, personality, intelligence, and what not,

Almost every possible crisis,

Hence the fascination for boys, for validation,

I'm empathetic to this category, really sad cases,

One of my many failures,

Despite my best efforts, I could never make her a strong lady.

I know you are in love,

I know you've always been in love with me,

Still, I'm sick of your fake, imaginary world,

I'm not possessive dear,

Just a bit of discipline, common sense, boundaries,

I can't afford a 'social embarrassment ' as my wife, mother of my kids,

So, farewell, I'm going.

Goodbye, someday you'll realise the truth,

In fact, you've realised it; I know you repent your attitude now, but late,

It's over now, no respect left, hence no love remaining, I'm sorry, heart.

Then there are the 'Crafty ones', my favourites,

Have had enough of them, tricky topics of the curriculum,

A must have experience if you want to cover the entire syllabus,

Ah me, how cruel!

How insensitive! How manipulative!

Somehow many of them without brothers,

And if they don't have father as well,

Then God protect you! So cold they are,

These 'Gamesters' have always disliked me,

As they would be deceived in judging the book by its cover.

Your turn first, madam, my usual approach,

Let me assess the depth of your faculties, let's see how potent your intellect is,

Then just one stroke, conclusive,

Chapter finished, game over, goodbye,

Your claim to be an expert in male psychology was on flimsy grounds,

Misplaced sense of confidence,

Sharpen your skills a bit sweetheart, next time.

And then the last ones, the 'Sweeties',

Good in academics, modest, disciplined, respectful to seniors,

Friendly, lively, smiling,

A priceless gem to the elders, pride of all associates,

They can belong to all categories mentioned above,

As and when desired, a bit of all of the above,

They keep on changing their looks as per the occasion,

They know the merits and demerits of each category,

They are always the best wives, finest mothers,

If you see manners in a kid, rest assured, mother has been such a girl only.

There might be combinations as well,

Some new, unknown categories too,

But the majority are covered in the above types,

All categories have beauty of their own,

You can have your preferences,

Yet you never know for whom you'll fall,

And if you fall for the wrong one,

All gates of hell break open.

25. Confidence

I'm a college teacher of blooming young boys and girls,

I care for their well-being, Concerned and affectionate too,

In fact, I love them,

With minimal expectation, if not unconditionally.

These restless souls earnestly desire confidence,

Most sought-after virtue!

Sometimes I really wonder, what, precisely, is confidence.

Perhaps, it's belief in one's abilities,

Accepting oneself without self-pity;

I'm what I am, For better or worse,

A humble defiance, to all judgements!

Some blessings, some misfortunes I'm born with;

Capitalising on my blessings, working upon my limitations,

Gradually I'm improving.

With every passing hour,

I'm adding new abilities, new skills, new knowledge, to my being,…

Trying, striving, moving, without ever comparing with others;

I proceed, like a perpetual learner.

Reflecting, introspecting, and growing,

I sense confidence approach slowly,

Not pride, just a soothing self-assurance,

Confidence is nothing but faith in the road taken,

No one is perfect;

As long as we are trying to improve, we deserve confidence,

It's a kind of courage to face the world,

And clarity about our place, the rightful place, in the creation.

Opinion of the world doesn't matter beyond a point,

If we please some, some others we always disappoint,

Our individuality is actually our essence,

Self-respect eventually leads to confidence!

26. One-sided Love

I've always been fascinated by one-sided love,

In fact, it's the destiny of majority of middle-class boys,

And I'm no exception to this punishment of Karma!

'Mutual love' option comes but rarely to lesser mortals like me,

If ever, just for a few days, for a couple of weeks if extremely lucky;

As a passing whim of sweet damsels,

Nowadays things might be different,

But in our times, 'Class' of the boys, used to be the decisive factor,

Naturally always disqualified at the prelims level!

The popular estimation was,

Friend zone, not datable!

Or datable only, not marriageable!

Sometimes just a fine substitute for solitude;

Frequently, an object, an entertainment, a romantic commodity.

So the uncouth social embarrassments,

Invariably prepared for UPSC,

The lucky ones getting their dream girls.

Commerce meeting Chemistry!

First, we were friends, and then it got converted into love!

Frequent announcements,

I could never experience such divine conversions!

Even in my distant imagination, I can never fall in love
with my friend.

Naturally, if ever, something came my way,

It was the ecstatic one-sided love,

Quite often, the much celebrated 'Love at first sight' for
me!

At the slightest encouragement, I'd let my imagination fly,

A seasoned expert in 'flight of fantasy',

Images of crushes would flash throughout the day,

Even an ordinary dame would appear a paragon of beauty,

I wish I could tell her,

That God's stock of beauty exhausted after your creation,
dear!

Listening to songs, on repeat mode,

Replacing the lead actor with the besotted lover,

Actresses substituted with the 'love interest'

Racing heartbeats without any rhyme or reason,

Studies going for a toss, no regret for academic loss,

Books can wait, not romance!

Transported to the world of imagination,

Daydreams and foolish confessions,

Imaginary stories, fanciful concoctions,

The sweetheart, the central figure, hardly concerned,

Her lover being a non-existent entity for her!

And the boy head over heels,

Even possessive without any tangible grounds,

Sometimes even proposals made,

And the rejection and mortifications!

Thank heavens, I'm no longer young!

The castle of romance crashing like a pack of cards!

Truly, fools rush in where angels fear to tread.

In a couple of months' time, normalcy restored,

But very soon, another story begins!

Yes, once again, one-sidedly!

Occasionally, maybe mistakenly, some mutuality would be visible,

Naturally, no academic activity for months,

Time beautifully spent in lazy delusions!

Yet, I cannot deny the bliss of these unproductive stories,

They had their own charm!

At least there is something to remember,

Inexhaustible fodder for pleasing digressions in leisure.

Something to smile about, no regret at all!

Otherwise, also, what's there in life?

Whether single or double!

It took me some years to realise,

That a man-woman relation is essentially of appetite,

A bit of chemistry only, lots of commerce,

As marriage is a social institution,

Love, at best, a habit or else a psychological malady.

Still, even to this day, the heart sometimes ignores the call of reasons,

And I still respond with the same juvenile idiocy!

Otherwise, a middle-class boy is officially allowed,

Only a romantic date with books,

Thick, heavy, boring! Eternal enemies of happiness.

Spoiling pleasure of vacation,

Frequently destroyers of festive occasions.

Presently I must confess, frankly and faithfully,

That to all the lovely ladies of the past, my one-sided soulmates,

I owe a genuine debt of gratitude, for giving me so many beautiful moments,

The cause might be artificial, but the pleasure was real,

Let there be sweet delusions and deceptive romantic creativity,

Defying logic, and all kinds of dull rationality,

Let there be deliberate confusion, imaginary notions,

Please do not deprecate, kindly do not mock,

The perpetual optimists, the lovers of one-sided chemistry!

27. Self-realisation

24th year of life,

Nine o'clock in the morning,

Tranquil heart feeling unexplained callings,

Some kids playing in the field,

Silently watching the game, yet lost in reflection,

A troubled soul trying to find solution.

Sudden explosion!

Somewhere in between both the eyes,

Like opening of a gate,

Connected to someone sitting very high in the sky!

Pure bliss, intellectual ecstasy, the highest peak of pleasure!

Mind floating in the universe,

A voice coming again from the same part of forehead,

Three worlds' monarch! Couldn't comprehend the meaning,

A human Sun, man becoming time,

And time losing relevance, just a flat surface static,

Possible to go back and forth,

Past and future irrelevant, events repeated in precise
sequence,

Just the present matters.

Love, logic, imagination or continence?

Precise reason, not sure,

Maybe a blend of these efforts, maybe divine design,

Maybe a reward for welfare intent,

Maybe something else.

Connected to the supreme being,

Yes, soul meeting the source,

Belief becoming knowledge,

And the brief encounter! Ah, me! Eternally grateful.

Scared a bit, actually,

Something, somewhere, is not okay.

And then the challenge, and the difficult choices, right
decision taken,

After six hours of knocking of death, some difficult tests
somehow cleared,

Unbearable pain, action losing control of reason,

Somehow managing to keep poised,

Nature attacking with full might,

Concern for the loved ones motivating to fight,

Chose to defy death till the last,

Will power and courage summoned,

Death is not an option, quickly realised,

Let's show steel.

Death defeated in three days; it was tough,

But the repercussions!

Fatal battles for a couple of weeks, decisions taken in
fraction of seconds,

Matrix of sound, even the responsibility to create
moments,

Supernatural warfare, angels and devils both active,

But had to fight alone,

By God's grace, all battles won!

Exposed to different times, some really interesting,

As if someone had a Time Machine,

No one dies realised, death is just a transition,

Soul is truly immortal.

Many secrets of Creation revealed,

Amusing, entertaining, delightful,

What pleasure, what excitement!

And then interaction with the 'One', the Father, the Ruler, the King!

Manhood in its finest garb,

Character and charisma! Who was he? No answer.

Absolute brilliance, electrifying humour,

What a man!

Brutal, fair, sensitive and dutiful,

No wonder all debts are ultimately paid,

Karma, to be precise!

And the beauty was, never a shirker!

Love and loyalty personified.

Yet a disillusioned smile, unfortunately, reason visible.

Finally, validation of efforts and compliments,

A big relief, life redefined.

Blissful experience,

Which makes everything material pointless,

Now clarity about life,

Little bit of strivings,

To make this world a better place,

What else?

Now salvation awaited,

Quite possible now,

God is the only player, thankfully.

A panacea for all the ills,

Now a hope for eternal bonds, possibly two cases,

It's a big number, it seems,

A conviction to like solitude,

Immediate family not needed,

Just a self-seeking survival technique,

Not a must, it's been confirmed, again very relieving!

No one is actually indispensable,

If they love, they will always be there, in all the births,

What's the anxiety for?

Just be a lover from your side,

Reciprocity will be tested after death,

Infinitely grateful to the Almighty,

Deep reverence.

Perennial peace and contentment, freedom from haste,

Really life is beautiful,

And God is the master artist!

28. Success

The results are out,

First-year over,

Two of my dear students made me proud!

My worthy favourites!

Others also must have done well,

Some more messages awaited.

Both the girls are sharp,

But this is not the reason for my bias,

Actually, they are very sincere,

Regular, focussed, hard-working and disciplined,

Mature enough to avoid unnecessary alliances,

Costing time, money, studies and emotional turbulences.

Maybe they are clear about 'life' and 'success'!

Success is nothing but our 'social worth',

All other romantic notions of success are reverse of
common sense,

"Success for me is mental peace," I've heard few wise men say,

What stupidity, what glamorous idiocy!

Social worth dear, nothing else.

Money, status, family, physicality, personality and fame,

There are no other parameters,

Life is mercilessly fair,

Quality of the partner, and so happiness, our social worth decides,

No confusion regarding this, please,

Ultimately this rule only prevails!

Besides, wealth to fulfil desires,

Cars, dresses, esteem and confidence,

Everything comes with social worth,

Don't ever imagine that you'll get more than you deserve, my dearest,

There is no injustice in society in this regard, at least.

Let's take an informed decision,

Now enjoy the so-called 'college life'!

Brutal truth will mock you very soon,

Been there, done that, faced the consequences,

First-hand experience, no secondary research friends!

Kindly flirt with time at your own peril.

Hence the importance of academic excellence!

Especially for service class kids.

Or else business,

And opening a grocery shop is not business!

If you earn less than two lakhs per month in a business,

Then you are doing a boring private job only.

Please don't make a mockery of business.

Let's not discuss other alternatives,

As they are not common.

And it's still not a success,

Just a tolerable existence.

Success means whether your opinion matters or not in society,

The relevance of your opinion at the national or international level,

Decides the magnitude of your success,

All other perceptions are just enticing mirages,

There is nothing wrong with having a comfortable survival,

But please don't call it success.
· 94 ·

For me, success is the only thing meaningful,

In this otherwise pointless life,

Truth however bitter,

Is always sweeter than blissful ignorance,

Let there be no invitation to travails,

And the respect for hard work prevails!

29. The Lessons of College Life

The college opening again, very soon,

New flowers waiting to bloom in the garden,

Old ones with added colour and fragrance!

Memories of my own college life flashes,

Mixed feelings of an ambitious boy,

Of a confused mind, a troubled heart,

The enquiry begins,

About life, love, society, relationships,

Here are the conclusions,

Some sweet, others not so sweet.

I realised that success is the pivot,

Around which a man's life revolves,

The tangibles matter not the aesthetics,

Achievements only, everything else cosmetics,

For the kids of service class parents,

Academics, the only capital,

Study-table the only friend,

Yet there was beauty in mooching around with friends,

Dutiful evening visits to all the places of youthful adventures,

And the social responsibility of offering attention and admiration!

In the endless debates, and animated discussions.

That love is a reality,

But a successful love story is a rare possibility,

As beyond fulfilment of appetite, relationships need commitment,

Close to prophetic principles!

So, normally instincts and materiality dominate relationships,

Once in a blue moon, companionship or chemistry,

Romance survives mainly in imagination, quite often just a tool of fantasy,

Yet the fatal charms of dames, refuse to die down despite years,

Maybe they're still the finest of God's creation.

That intelligence lies in creativity,

Field of enquiry doesn't matter;

There is no difference between Einstein and Shakespeare,

Plato and Picasso, Newton and Rousseau,

Are all alike, equally able!

Brilliance is not cramming facts or clearing an entrance,

All jobs, though necessary, are but traps,

Exams are designed for academic labourers primarily,

Test of hard work, mindless speed and mechanical abilities,

Sophisticated glorification of mediocrity,

Yet there is a thrill in academics,

Indeed, there is a sense of achievement in decoding its
tricks and secrets,

Please note, failure is not an option.

Excellence is not a slave of destiny, but success is.

As it's acknowledgement of society, and society is not
always rational or fair,

Hence the relevance of chance,

Yet, luck deceives, but not always!

So, by and large, efforts matter.

Yet a day well spent is a success,

An evening full of laughter, a night of ease,

Is nothing but success.

That confidence is insensitivity toward public opinion,

Negation of all judgements, all expectations,

It's faith in the path chosen,

Good or bad, right or wrong,

We're accountable only to God,

So, we're here to live and let live,

Beyond courtesy, all expectations, are intrusion into
privacy,

Yet people are essentially good,

Eighty per cent beauty, some absolute beauty, the rest a
possibility.

That personality is to be alive,

A functional heart, an active mind, a bit of conscience,

Charm lies in being natural,

Humility begets humour, observation supplies wit,

Life is not something to be taken seriously,

The summary is,

To give pleasant moments to fellow beings,

Everything else is meaningless, momentary,

Personality is simplicity,

Just taking it easy.

That for a middle-class boy, survival is the issue,

Life, satisfaction, fulfilment, creative pleasure,

All these are just fancy talks,

An empty stomach knows no creativity, there is no grace in poverty,

Whether we like it or not, there is beauty in affluence!

Life begins only when the basics are done,

Hence, the importance of jobs, the barest minimum first.

That happiness is a reaction to circumstances,

If we wait for it, it comes but rarely,

An occasional episode in the regular drama of monotony,

I'll have to make efforts to be happy,

The easiest is to make others laugh.

That God is the only player,

And I have to enact the role assigned,

One day we all have to face the music of karma,

The presence of Almighty is the ultimate relief,

All trials come to an end someday.

Salvation, freedom from the cycle of death and birth,

Might dawn with all its beauty and bliss someday.

30. When you ignore me...

When you ignore me,

My heart goes sinking,

Disturbing is the feeling,

Silent tears come on my cheeks,

I suffer for weeks,

It cuts me to the quick,

Oh dear, when you ignore me.

There was a time when you loved me,

When you lovingly touched me,

When everything was 'ours',

And you'd talk to me for hours,

What's happened now dear?

How coldly you treat me now.

When you ignore me,

Silent tears come on my cheeks,

I suffer for weeks,

It cuts me to the quick,

Oh dear, when you ignore me.

When I see you with someone else,

My world crumbles down,

My heart breaks,

And I am down,

Thousand bruises I feel,

Which no one can heal,

I feel so low and weak.

When you ignore me,

Silent tears come on my cheeks,

I suffer for weeks,

It cuts me to the quick,

Oh dear, when you ignore me.

Oh dear, when you ignore me.

31. When you look at me

When you look at me,

My heart goes beating,

It's such a beautiful feeling,

I feel there's love, yes there is love,

Oh dear, when you look at me.

Your smile and the rays,

Your eyes and the glaze,

Your cheeks and the blaze,

Your talks and the rage,

And the tresses gleaming,

When you look at me,

My heart goes beating,

It's such a beautiful feeling,

I feel there's love, yes there is love,

Oh dear, when you look at me.

Your charms with courtesies,

Your face, and its beauties,

Your dresses with subtleties,

Your glances of perplexities,

Communications, a bit baffling,

When you look at me,

My heart goes beating,

It's such a beautiful feeling,

I feel there's love, yes there is love,

Oh dear, when you look at me.

When I'm alone, I react,

I doubt and reflect,

I think and introspect,

With a trembling heart, in fact,

Is it love or a wishful thinking?

Yet sweetheart, when you look at me,

My heart goes beating,

It's such a beautiful feeling,

I feel there's love, yes there is love,

Oh dear, when you look at me.

Oh dear, when you look at me.

32. Friends

When we have a joke to share,

Or we've to discuss a mademoiselle sweet;

When we need a confidant,

Or want analysis of racing heartbeat;

When we intend to enter into a discussion,

Forgetting all repercussions;

When we don't want to hold our tears,

And willing to confess all our fears;

Only few arms we wish to depend,

Yes, it's the cosy company of loving friends!

Parents give us life,

Friends give meaning to life;

Whatever little bit of pleasure I know,

I owe it all to my friends,

We might not meet regularly,

Yet, they're an irreplaceable part of my destiny,

The sweetest of all relations!

God sent angels to add charm to life,

Smile, giggle and naughty laughter,

It's because of them, whether now or hereafter,

Dear buddies, whenever we've parted our ways,

A part of me has always gone away!

33. When you walk with me

When you walk with me,

God, you and your fragrance!

Who has the time to look at moons and stars?

They all lose relevance!

There is excitement and racing heartbeats,

It's really a destiny's treat!

There's thrill in your company,

I see nothing other than you,

You, your dress, your tresses, your smile,

Everything so captivating!

Yes, sweetheart,

When you walk with me,

Oh dear, when you walk with me.

Your words are so warm,

And my wish to hold you in arms!

Where should I look at?

In your beautiful eyes,

Or at your rosy face?

When you walk with me,

Oh, dear when you walk with me.

You are frank but my hesitation,

You are calm but my awkward attention,

My silence but genuine attachments,

Everything clumsy but a beautiful combination.

Is this love I ask when alone,

But there is no answer,

Just a haunting silence.

She is your soulmate you fool,

So just go ahead,

My heart sometimes assures me,

And I'm encouraged to say,

Let's walk again baby,

And then I'd say,

When you walk with me,

There's love, there's chance,

There's chemistry, there's romance.

34. Love- II

When the journey seems tough,

And the heart is sick of trials;

When you swim against the current,

Yet, there are disturbing denials;

When the spirit is low,

And you feel like calling it a day,

I'm just a phone call away.

When you're trying to resolve complications,

And life seems to be in a mess;

When there is displeasing dilemma,

Or unwanted stress;

When you just want a company,

Though, you don't have much to say,

I'm just a phone call away.

When you feel intellectual ecstasy,

And want expression;

When there is a victory,

And you want celebration;

When the cupid strikes,

And you want clarity without delay,

I'm just a phone call away.

Now you are on your own,

In a city unknown,

A man in the making,

Far away from home;

Principles, discipline and academic excellence,

Will make you a being of some significance;

Come what may, don't accept mediocrity,

Excellence is the only virtue, everything else sophistry!

35. Mr Upendra Prasad

(Our Hindi Teacher)

A simple man with decent attire,

A lovely teacher we always admired;

Profound knowledge, brilliant teaching style,

Affectionately friendly, tolerated us with smile.

One thing he would stress always,

That you should have your 'own' language;

Selection of words was to score the key,

This is how it seemed to me.

Sometimes he would quote Shelley and Keats,

Sometimes Wordsworth and other romantics;

Now I realise language doesn't come smoothly,

And it's not just vocabulary, metaphor and simile.

He would discuss psychology, philosophy and whatnot!

I still can't decide whether to listen or make a note;

God wanted to teach us life, language and creativity,

Hence, he sent Mr Upendra Prasad, a thorough gentleman,
if not a divinity!

36. Suban

It's your birthday today,

Nothing new to tell you,

We all know,

You are sharp, sweet and sensitive,

Lively, witty and sufficiently mature,

But the beauty is,

You're sincere too!

It's really pleasing to see,

That you understand,

The necessity of discipline and hard work,

Let me tell you one thing,

Science is fascinating, needless to say,

But so are humanities,

Equally fascinating are languages,

Hindi as well as English.

A complete man is possible,

If he is equally proficient,

In all the fields of human enquiry,

All knowledge is beautiful,

There is nothing easy or difficult, great or small.

Life is all about skills,

The more, the merrier!

But above all,

True education makes us humble,

Courteous, well-mannered and a lover.

Life is a mixed bag,

Full of good things,

Bad things too!

We become what we choose,

We are what we decide to be.

Our birthday reminds us,

That we're here for some purpose,

Life is all about finding that purpose,

And to continue to be the person you are now,

Charming, genuine, lovely,

Friendly, laughing and manly.

37. Mr R N Singh

(Our English Teacher)

A handsome man with charming face,

Poet like sensitivity, divine grace;

Genuineness personified, aura dignified,

Serious demeanour, enough to terrify.

Punctual, purposeful and stylish teacher,

A believer in setting example, never a preacher;

With mischievous smile, he introduced phonetics,

Later we realised it was one of his beautiful tactics.

The words he taught, still haunt many of his pupils,

We couldn't be Wordsworth, yet literary sense is in us instilled;

Simple writing, he always encouraged,

Pompous expressions were not tolerated;

A skilful teacher with beauty and perfection,

Difficult to substitute in ages to come!

When strangers find us proficient in language,

And are surprised to read in English our musings;

We all, with elation and victorious smile, announce,

We have the blessing of being taught by Mr R N Singh!

38. Misconception

I thought competition was all about knowledge,

Alas, it's hard-work and speed!

I was quite mistaken.

I thought success was academics,

Ah me, it's mastery of a skill!

I was really mistaken.

I thought happiness was about money,

Oh God, it's satisfaction and mental peace!

I was profoundly mistaken.

I thought love was a reality,

Ah, it's just a psychological delusion!

I was mightily mistaken.

I thought friendship lasted forever,

Ah me! There is poison of status!

As usual, I was substantially mistaken.

Likewise, I had a faulty notion about many things,

Beauty, achievement, relations and fun,

In fact, about life itself!

As time goes by,

I'm trying to refine my perceptions,

Majorly, the issues are settled,

But, sometimes, perhaps it's too late to mend,

Yet I've decided to fight till death,

Come what may,

I've to be the victor someday;

And, God willing, I may have the last laugh.

Still, every day I see young boys and girls,

With similar whims and fancies,

Deliberately I keep silent.

Sometimes, it's nice to be blissfully ignorant,

Sometimes, clarity brings disillusionment,

Let the heart occasionally ignore the call of prudence,

Let's not allow wisdom,

To crush the child within us,

And do not let it fetch us,

The boring gravity and gloomy silence.

39. Tejas

God sent a flower, to rid us from gloom,

Delightful it is, to watch it bloom;

Dad's ambition, mother's pride,

To me just a sweetheart, a relief and to

Confide…

A jolly, bright boy, explores life's complexities,

Sensitive and reflective, modern with courtesies;

Boyish appeal, expressive eyes,

With pretty damsels, canny, subtle guise!

Popular ambitions, desirous of being affluent,

Mischievous temperament, naughty undercurrent;

Heart in sports, movies and music,

Gradually relishing intoxications of academics;

Briskly his perceptions become accurate,

Training himself to be diligent and sedate.

A sharp observer possesses aesthetic prudence,

Keen mind, with sophisticated eloquence;

I wish he becomes a man of merit,

In time's tests shows, character and grit;

If possible, O God, give him fulfilment and success,

This is my prayer for our heartbeat, Tejas!

40. Miss S...

Few months back, we missed the chance of conversation,

So, let's take refuge in memory on this occasion;

It's not easy to assess the personality from childhood impressions,

Yet the basics never change; what alter is polish and sophistication;

A charming face and pleasing smile I can vividly recollect,

Incentive enough for some of us to adjust timing and to wait.

Girlish appeal, downcast eye, delicate constitution,

Reserved and sensible she seemed on observation;

Simple and genuine on further analyses,

A young lady who can keep her composure in life's crises.

Presently she is enjoying the marital bliss,

As a lovely wife with kids of promise;

A life full of simple pleasures, togetherness and gaiety,

Is my wish for the young lady graceful and pretty!

41. Shobha Ma'am

(Our History Teacher)

Mrs Shobha Pandey was the only Ma'am who taught us,

Unlike modern schools, where situation is quite the reverse;

One day we heard, "A new teacher is coming for History!"

We were thrilled after being told that she was a lady!

History was being made by a history teacher!

I still vividly recollect her demeanour and poise,

Her lovely white sari, fair complexion and nervous sweet voice.

She was a bit apprehensive initially,

All the teachers know this profession is not that cushy;

Very hard-working and sincere teacher, I would opine,

Meticulously made notes and lecture delivery fine;

She was tender, incapable of berating the naughty elements,

Still, she commanded respect due to her commitment.

Nowadays, to be a feminist is in fashion,

Which is nothing but male animadversion;

To me, Shobha Ma'am epitomises feminism,

She came to a far-off place, away from her family;

Independent, affectionate to students and fulfilling conjugal responsibilities,

What else is, after all, womanhood or for that matter, manhood?

A blend of beauty, intellect, decency and simplicity,

Despite struggles she possesses, positivity and jollity;

Even today, there is girlish sprightliness and love for work,

Even to this day, we can feel her vivacity and graceful spark!

42. Mr Anshuman Chatterjee

(Our History Teacher)

A perfect teacher to teach us history,

With whom we had affectionate chemistry;

One of the most good-looking teachers I ever had,

Whose presence was always a reason to make us glad;

Skilled sportsman, accomplished musician, and passionately loved academics.

Friendly, warm, lively and fine aesthetics,

Always concerned about our well-being and career;

My friends made him proud by becoming bureaucrats and engineers,

I oft think, have I let him down by not qualifying for an IAS?

My heart tells me, at least try to emulate him and be a teacher with the least bias!

Life is just an aggregate of experiences, I sometimes believe,

Mr Anshuman Chatterjee will surely remain a beautiful
one as long as we live!

On his birthday, I wish him health and amusement in life,

Love from students and offspring and companionship with
wife!

43. Mr Diwakar Mishra

(*Our Music Teacher*)

Mastery over craft,

A man committed to art;

Life of rhythm and beats,

His classes were always a treat.

Strict disciplinarian,

Master musician;

A tough teacher to his pupils,

A versatile man with varied skills,

A charming, warm man and a lover of life,

Full of energy and lovely smile;

Whenever I hear the beats of Tabla,

I am sweetly reminded of Mr Diwakar Mishra!

44. Mataji

Initial days in Vikram House, whereas teens we've grown,

My bed adjoining window, opening in Shrimanji's lawn;

'Aayega aanewala' we heard one evening,

How thrilled we were, how captivating!

What a beautiful voice and perfect rendition,

As good as Lataji and there is no exaggeration!

It was sheer delight listening to her melodious singing,

A pleasant interruption to our academic musings;

Frank, natural, responsible and warm,

Modern, lively, vigilant with motherly charm;

And the chemistry between Shrimanji and his adoring wife,

A sweet lady who loves and lives life;

Briskly time flies and now she is a bit mellow,

Still affectionate and braving destiny's flow;

May God give her health, spirit, grit, and glee,

This is the wish to our lovely Mataji!

45. Shrimanji

(*R. G. Marathe/Warden*)

Not an easy occasion to write on,

Lot many memories in mind flash upon;

Was father of two kids and fatherly to some teens mischievous,

Those childhood moments are really precious.

Disciplinarian, he was and a man so courageous,

Outwardly tough, from within humorous;

Romantic he was, we all know, and modern in outlook,

His psychological tests, how can we overlook?

He is not with us, he must be looking from above,

Bestowing blessings from the vicinity of God and lots of love!

46. The Contradiction

There was a time when I was young,

I think I was a nice boy then and loved life;

I had an opinion about all the issues of life,

And I believed I had taken the right path,

But alas, I was mightily mistaken!

Friendship, I thought,

was attachment and loyalty;

But, to my surprise, it was network and utility,

Love, I believed, was chemistry and connect,

Unfortunately, it was everywhere, coins and contacts;

Intelligence, it was my conviction, lay in reflection and creation,

But there it was, to memorise for recitation.

Personality, for me, was frankness and originality,

But, there I observed, it was affectation and formality;

Academics, I believe, is to contribute to the knowledge pool,

But there it was nothing, beyond a degree to look cool!

Beauty, ideally, should please a sense of aesthetics,

There, by and large, it was to appeal to instincts;

Modernity lies in open-mindedness and humility,

There it was, to outsmart and sophisticated hypocrisy.

Wherever I went and whatever I saw,

There always lay a subtle contradiction;

Maybe my intellect failed to analyse precisely,

Or maybe my perceptions failed to reach maturity;

Whatever be reason, the contradiction still goes on,

And I'm left as a silent observer,

Smiling but alone!

47. Dad's Daughters

When I see a fine girl,

Modest, courteous, feminine,

Of spotless eyes, genuine,

Unlike embittered feminists,

Invariably I think about her father.

A warm lady or a tender girl,

Is always a father's daughter,

Conditioned and nurtured by her loving dad,

The father-daughter bond seems to me paradisiacal,

The finest of all human relations,

Perhaps the only source of unconditional love for women.

The hapless father knows,

She is not an investment for old age,

She'll go away one day,

In a new family, among new relatives,

Her priorities will change,

Father-in-law, rather than the father bereft of law!

His position changing from central to peripheral,

Essential to a feel-good factor,

Still, his daughter is the world for him,

Carrying her school bag, tying shoelaces,

Guiding, cautioning, disciplining,

Telling do's and don'ts,

Trying patiently to make her a good girl.

And secretly conscious of the day of farewell,

Of adieu, the final goodbye,

Still, every moment concerned for his daughter,

Sad in her sufferings, ecstatic in her success,

Heaven, what a relationship this is!

A beautiful display of human selflessness,

Of prophetic character, human perfection!

This dad-daughter relation,

Is an absolute beauty,

A continual source of perpetual bliss!

Sometimes I feel if ever a man gets love from a woman,

She has to be his own heart moving,

In the shape of a lovely daughter!

• 139 •

48. Chemistry

I'm a chemistry graduate,

It's my first love in academic sense,

Natural as well as human chemistry,

Interesting as a subject, intriguing as an issue,

Man-women relation and it's chemistry,

What a beautiful shade of life!

Chemistry beautifies relationships,

Wherever love sparkles, there's chemistry,

Silent communications through heartbeats,

By a glance, a touch, or just silence,

Messages exchanged effortlessly,

Soul supplied to dry commitments,

Spice to tasteless tales,

Distinctive flavours to connections,

Charm to dull obligations,

Thrills to sensations, kicks of intoxication!

When I see a couple,

Young or old, modern or traditional,

I quickly mark the intensity of the pull,

Flood of valentines,

Alas, the chemistry missing!

Instincts dominating the game,

Brute play of words, stale expressions dancing,

Actions without conviction, insincerity of confessions,

Husbands, nothing but social toys,

Woman, a trophy wife!

Where there is chemistry,

There is life;

Morning a bliss, evenings occasion for tryst,

Romance in the morn, companionship at night,

Glow on the face,

Adorning beauty with grace,

Monotony sublimating, without any trace,

Troubles evaporating, now,

tolerable the rat race!

Let's explore love and its mysteries,

Let there be ecstasy,

Let there be chemistry!

49. Raksha Bandhan

Once again, this lovely festival has come,

As a child, I used to be thrilled on this occasion;

When I grew up, I started dreading it,

Because now we have to add tangibility to emotions.

Sisters assess us most leniently,

And perhaps the only source of unconditional love;

Rakhi reminds us of our duty to protect them,

But beyond a point, all brothers are as helpless as a dove;

Brothers' success is sisters' success,

Brother's suffering is a reason for their distress,

Where else do you find such heart-to-heart camaraderie!

Today we brothers are here to assert,

That we may not call you frequently or visit your place,

Yet you are always there in our consciousness,

Maybe we are avoiding unnecessary intrusion in your space.

Childhood fights we still cherish,

Your achievement we are still proud of,

And shortcomings we have forgotten long ago,

Just give your best to your blessed partners,

And keep remembering your equally blessed brothers.

50. Miss M…

Chemistry class is going on,

Pupils not interested in the lecture,

Suddenly comes Miss M… with all her beauty and power,

What an antidote to bear the lecture!

All male faces start glowing now,

And a soothing fragrance occupies,

All the dull corners of the theatre,

Tall, appealing, and lovely hair,

Chubby cheeks and complexion fair,

Natural personality, a young lady genuine,

Energy, elan and pretty sanguine,

Friendly, amiable and quite helpful,

Comes to college in dresses colourful.

People come and go,

So are the classmates,

But the picture we paint on the canvas of heart,

Remains forever.

And only through these pictures,

We know each other,

And meet daily with silent communication.

51. Conclusions of the Forties

Life starts at 40,

Somewhere I read, couldn't believe it though;

Thought life ends at forty: no youth, less energy, more disillusionments;

Yet I reflected on its meaning,

Maybe the author meant the experience we have at that age,

And indeed, financial security;

So here are my conclusions.

First, happiness is a mirage,

An occasional episode in the usual monotonous drama;

It's better to seek it in mental peace, good work and learning to enjoy solitude;

Satisfaction is the foundation of happiness,

And I've to make efforts to be happy;

The best way is to make others happy.

Then love is a figment of imagination,

A rare emotion,

As it requires principles and sacrifice;

Yet it's a necessity, a continual need;

And all human beings are open to it,

We are all blessed with the faculty of discretion,

So love and genuineness have universal appeal.

Further, I realised money is necessary,

And efforts must be made to earn as much as it's possible by fair means;

Yet it's not a sufficient condition for happiness.

All pleasures of life,

Comes from meaningful relationships,

Whether friends, family or partner,

There's no other source.

Besides, I realised,

Women can't love the way men love them;

Their love lies in their mind, not in the heart,

And they express it through respect and admiration;

They may become emotionally attached,

Yet that doesn't qualify a man to be her lifelong
companion;

Nothing wrong with this,

This is the way they are made by nature.

Then I also realised that life is all about skills,

And it comes with persistent hard work;

Intelligence has little role to play in it.

The more skills one has,

The more successful he becomes;

And for men, success is the only thing relevant,

Everything else has just cosmetic utility.

Then I learnt to acknowledge the dignity of work,

No work is big or small,

As long as it's done in the best possible way,

And nothing can match the feeling of contentment,

After finishing a job well.

One other important conclusion is,

That more than animals and environment,

Human beings should be treated well;

A being with mind and heart,

Require delicate handling;

And tolerance comes by focusing,

On the merits of individuals,

Which everyone possesses some;

Now I believe that education is reflected,

In how we treat others;

After all, courtesy costs nothing.

Finally, in the forties,

I became clear about the spiritual realm;

About self-realisation and salvation, deeds and karma,

Time, destiny and free will and about human limitations;

I realised life is eternal, endless, perpetual,

This is only the world in transition;

There is indeed an Almighty,

The King, the Master, the Ruler;

And it's really quite relieving to know this.

So, I've no desire to be young again,

With many faults of nature then;

In the grip of sentimentality and passion;

With efforts and God's grace, I'm a bit calm now;

True, I'm no longer young and quite bereft of youthful
appeal,

Still, I've the advantages of mature years;

With little bit of money and a comfortable survival,

I'm inclined to believe that,

Life really starts at 40.

52. Falling in Love

Love is an interesting topic,

Appeals to all men, irrespective of age;

A time comes for us when the only thing worth
remembering,

Is our 'love interest' in the past;

Everything else eventually loses charm.

There was a time when I used to make fun of love;

I thought it's an illusion, a psychological malady!

But it's a reality, in fact, a beautiful reality;

Men do fall in love;

An intriguing, complex emotion!

Even women fall in love, but their approach to it is
different,

Due to social conditioning, they are trained to take
precautions,

To look for security, to apply mind in the matters of heart;

'To be or not to be' is their perpetual dilemma.

Ultimately it makes love an enigmatic mystery.

A man-woman relation is not merely physical,

Fortunately, there is more to it;

You see a face, and there is a magnetic attraction;

Biology is the last thing that comes to mind;

Just her presence is thrilling,

A glance is enough to keep you charged the whole day;

Music has new meaning to you;

Suddenly lyrics become relevant;

You begin enjoying solitude;

And you are happy without reason;

Her face and words haunt you;

One positive comment,

And you are in seventh heaven!

You forget home, even friends;

Transported into a blissful world.

There's another facet of love, the spiritual one;

If things materialise it gives you stability, mental peace,
happiness;

If it doesn't, it makes you detached;

Material world fails to impress you now, Geeta becomes clear.

Whether you accept me or not, just be happy and enjoy your life;

Though I know it's difficult, yet hopefully, you get someone,

Who loves you more than me; but there is a difference,

Between the care of husbands and commitment of a lover;

Still no grievances at all.

There is yet another aspect, the supernatural one!

Telepathic communication starts,

You can feel her presence despite the distance,

Sometimes even feel the heartbeat,

If the other party is undergoing the same emotions,

No wonder Catherine said in Wuthering Heights,

"I'm Heathcliff; he is always, always in my mind!"

Sometimes possession of the soul is possible,

Though it's a perfect torture; gross injustice to manhood,

Yet it happens, there is no point expecting,

Logic and sense of fairness from someone,

Who wants 'best of all worlds',

Need can be fulfilled, and greed is limitless,

Anyway, unison of man and woman; man and woman becoming one!

We all know the concept behind 'Shivalinga',

Maybe for the infinite eternity, if both agree,

Whether you succeed or fail in love,

It teaches you a thousand lessons,

That's why it's always better to have loved and lost,

Than never to have loved at all.

My time is over, thankfully,

Sometimes even hope is problematic,

When the road ends, there is silence,

Acceptance and submission to destiny,

You are finally reconciled to life,

Yet the heart is rebellious, and the desire never dies,

Feminine charm is lethal; never lose its deadly appeal,

So the planning for the other world starts,

Someone might be there waiting,

Where class, status, or family is meaningless,

Even time and age lose relevance there,

Only a loyal companion matters,

A sweetheart, a partner or a lover.

53. Good Boys

I'm a college teacher,

Naturally, I teach young boys and girls,

The batches are usually a mix of different characters,

Some boys are really good and sweet,

I'm a bit worried about them.

There are some sweet girls too,

But I'm hardly concerned about them,

Very soon, nature would make them flexible',

But as regards the 'good boys', I don't know.

There was a time I was myself a 'good boy',

Now I don't claim this adjective,

As now I'm exposed to all kinds of negativities.

Ignorance is no longer a bliss now; neither I'm a boy.

To be a 'good man' is tough, in fact, very tough!

Nowadays, I just do my duties and try to be fair.

So, let's talk about the new kids,

These boys are sensitive, silent and observant,

They just listen to the lecture,

And hesitant to participate in discussions,

Seem lost in their thoughts,

Trying to decode meaning of the world,

Maybe thinking how to adjust with modern times.

Now I can sense the struggles lying ahead of them,

Their friends may let them down,

Lovers may ask for the 'moon',

They may cease to be the parent's favourites,

Teachers may take side of 'smart' peers,

Society may conspire to make them someone else,

Their confidence may shake quite often;

They may have to inhale the poison of unrequited love,

And clouds of cynicism may envelop their beautiful soul,

Maybe endless strife on the road not taken.

Still every cloud has a silver lining,

And the situation is not that dismal,

They'll get 'personality' in return!

There is 'give and take' in nature,

Such species are God's favourite,

I'm sure God will protect them,

Their intellect would flower out,

And they would bloom into fine men,

Into a man of substance and purpose,

Creativity, the true measure of intelligence,

Would embrace them if they make little effort,

Sense of aesthetics may court them,

And someday, God Willing, they would become,

A beautiful and valuable asset of society.

54. Love & Duty

I was a great believer in love when young,

I thought people badly need it,

In books, movies, art, everywhere, there were talks of it,

Literature, poems, songs and paintings,

Replete with romantic sentiments,

Even teachers would paint an ideal picture of life,

A good human being should have a functional heart,

I was told,

Naturally, I continued to be a lover for a long time,

But alas! I was greatly mistaken.

My experiences told me,

Be it friendship, family or romance,

People don't mind being loved, but it's rarely a priority,

It's just a charming diversion, not something indispensable,

Just a sweet concept for fantasy, not to be put into practice,

Reading romantic novels, and watching romantic movies,

Is just a fashionable thing to indulge in,

Even falling in love for some 'experience' is something very much desirable.

But I've never seen 'love' as a matter of belief and principle,

The guiding tenets have always been 'utility' and 'relevance',

I've no intention to be cynical,

Yet I couldn't help observing this utilitarian principle,

Being applied to someone as close as parents too,

No wonder we belong to 'animal kingdom',

Some of us are by nature, emotional,

They are normally found to be continually suffering,

Or to be taken as a weak individual,

Quite often as ignorant 'simpletons'.

As I grew up, I realised that,

All relations are one-sided,

There is no point in expecting mutuality,

You never know what others are thinking,

Expectations of love, commitment, involvement, etc. lead to trouble,

It makes you prone to frequent heartbreaks,

Makes your life an unbearable obligation.

So it was necessary to find a solution to this reality,

I don't know how others cope with it,

After some deliberations, I decided to switch to 'duty',

With effort, I learnt to keep my sentiments in check,

And started focusing on my duty in every relationship,

And it works!

Not that I don't love my near and dear ones,

But I know it's immaterial,

Something peripheral, not of a great moment,

I wish I had known it when I was young!

It would have saved lots of my time, energy and wasted emotions,

Yet, as they say, "It's never too late to mend."

Despite this, presently, I see lots of hue and cry about love,

Proposals, acceptance, confessions and celebrations,

Love you and love you too!

No doubt I find it exciting,

But sometimes I wonder who these people are,

Getting love so easily, which appeared to me such an impossibility,

Then I'm forced to reflect,

Am I somewhere mistaken for my feeble reasons, or...

55. Love and Loyalty

I was in love once; with all my heart, I loved her,

She reciprocated my feelings and loved me too,

One day, I realised she valued someone else more,

Had respect for him, for his 'class' or maybe intelligence,

Still, she was willing to spend her life with me,

I guess she had feelings for me,

But I understood my true place,

I was actually the second choice.

I had a friend, a very good friend,

I loved him, we had lots of fun,

Time passed by and now he has new friends,

More successful than me and of more social utility,

We are still close friends, but now there is a change in priority,

Sadly, I realised that I'm no longer the first choice.

I loved my parents with all my heart and soul,

Perhaps more than my other siblings,

As I grew up, despite my best efforts, I became mediocre socially,

My parents still love me fondly, but I can't help realising the fact,

That here also, my mediocrity made me the second choice.

Now I'm a teacher, friendly and concerned; try to give my best,

And I love my pupils like I love other teens in my family,

But now I'm wise and know that relations are always one-sided,

You never know who'll reciprocate and how,

The degree and intensity of involvement never match,

Other's max might be your barest minimum,

We all want to be loved, but loving others is something we disapprove,

As it has some inherent risk uninsurable,

Besides, we want love from worthy individuals, not from every Tom, Dick, and Harry.

Now the question is, should I change my approach to life?

Or be happy being a second choice?

Is it also a kind of love and loyalty?

Or merely for convenience and expression of pity?

The issue is not yet settled,

Love is still an enigma, an unsolved puzzle.

56. Men, Women & Love

First men, I'm a bit confident about them,

Face: sometimes, physicality most of the time;

Intellect: rarely matters, if at all;

Academics: not at all;

Dressing sense: important issue majorly;

Sensibility: desirable though not indispensable;

Loyalty: don't take this issue lightly;

Submissiveness: old school necessity, not now;

Eyes: almost universal appeal;

Smile: for some observant few;

Voice: for some unique cases, it's an issue;

Rationality: they are mentally prepared for its rare presence;

Genuineness: highly valued, relevance in love comes with age;

Lastly, and importantly, if you ever mock a man,

It's advisable never to seek love and respect from him.

Now, women, it's a guess only;

Please ignore if you disagree;

Appearance: matters for a romantic few, otherwise just entertainment;

Personality: makes you datable, not marriageable;

Humour: universal appeal, you can safely rely on it;

Finance: let's not discuss this obvious issue;

Academics: hardly matters, in fact, something scary;

Smartness or worldly wisdom: most coveted trait undoubtedly;

Values and principles: appeals to them after 50;

Respect: initially a light issue, later the central concern;

Decency: appeals either to very young girls or senior ladies;

Dressing sense: for a chosen few only;

Loyalty: desirable, not indispensable;

Attachment: desirable but selectively;

Care: a must but again selectively;

Ah me, the mirage of 'selective' virtue!

Face, smile, voice, etc.: cosmetic utility only;

Submissiveness and patience: if you have this priceless virtue,

You're a sure winner with the ladies!

Poetry: please never reveal this talent;

A sincere suggestion, only advice I'm sure of;

Biology: not sure, perhaps the foundation of chemistry;

Status: more important than the candidate.

I agree above views are generalisations only,

And generalisation shows poor analysis.

For some men, emotional connect is the only thing that matters;

Sometimes a woman goes to extremes for the man she loves;

You never know what will appeal in a particular case;

Yet we try to decode a pattern in the given facts;

This is how theory evolves;

A theory never answers all questions;

Yet it enhances understanding;

Whatever be the truth,

Love is the foundation that sustains all relationships;

And ultimately, chemistry wins the race.

57. Modern Indian Women

Everyone needs a company,

But sometimes things don't materialise,

And Love's Labour is Lost!

Economics quite often outsmarts *Chemistry*.

Normally cynicism comes with failed relationships,

And we are prone to generalise,

And the entire gender is seen in poor light,

Yet when reason prevails,

We come back to our trusting, positive self.

Comparison is not a nice thing,

Not expected from a truly rational being,

Yet to put things in context,

When I observe the young women of modern times,

I see stark differences from those of my generation,

In personality, perceptions and preferences,

In spirit, behaviour and values too,

And there is no bias, just an objective assessment.

The first thing is that,

They have the clarity about what they want,

In life, from their partner and from their career,

Indeed, they value finance even today.

But it's not something indispensable now,

Money these days is secondary to personality,

Girls don't want dependence now,

Actually, a matter of self-respect!

Equal footing is the philosophy of modern women.

Then there is substantial proportion of genuine girls these days,

Natural, transparent, pristine,

Honest face and clear eyes, entirely guileless,

And surprisingly kind too!

Their dads are to be given credit for this,

Girls with cold, unfeeling fathers,

Are sometimes harsh to men,

And ruthlessness is always a matter of temperament, not of physicality.

Further, these modern women are unapologetic,

About their gender, background or even looks!

'I'm what I am', is the motto,

Least concerned about social judgement and public
opinion,

Frank, straightforward and confident,

Knowing how to be presentable and fine aesthetic sense,

A beautiful manifestation of womanhood.

Girls of our time, two decades back, were a bit
unfortunate, I think,

They had to strike a balance between tradition and
modernity,

And the society was a bit regressive then,

And by and large unfair to women,

Naturally, the soil was not conducive to beautiful flowers,

Still, no doubt, there were some roses and dahlias.

In all societies, majorly men sustain womanhood,

It was J. S. Mill who provided,

Intellectual foundation for the feminist movement,

In India, too, social ills with regard to women,

Were opposed initially by men only,

It's really heartwarming to see,

That Indian fathers have transformed a lot,

An assured source of unconditional love for women.

Our country is a 'developing' nation from the last so many years,

I genuinely believe that,

If ever it becomes 'developed',

The credit would go precisely,

To these Modern Indian Women,

After all, young modern men need a helping hand,

And are desperately searching for,

A loving friend, a caring companion and a lovely sweetheart.

58. Personality

A continual source of pleasure is human personality,

A fine man or a fine woman is an absolute beauty,

Even a nicely brought up young boy or a girl,

Is a blessing to society,

No doubt stars, clouds, flowers and moon are beautiful,

Yet there is a limitation to their appeal,

Human appeal is limitless.

Who can ever match the beauty of,

Wordsworth, Shakespeare or Milton,

Dinkar, Ghalib or Sahir,

Plato, Rousseau or Voltaire,

Brontes, Mary Shelley and other great ladies,

Civilisation has produced a multiplicity of scholars,

Artists, leaders and thinkers, even sportspersons,

Who never ceases to thrill us,

To inspire and entertain us.

Personality, we all know, is an attainment,

We are not born with this,

It's something to be cultivated,

I'm not a great believer in God's gift,

Maybe looks and vocal cords we get by birth,

Everything else is an accomplishment.

A charming man or a woman is not accidental,

Appearance or physicality has little role to play,

It might be an add-on,

What really matters is evolution of mind, heart and soul,

In other words,

Intellectual, emotional and spiritual growth,

The non-physical aspect!

Here lies the secrets of magnetism,

Of the appeal which is sustainable.

When we are young,

We are drawn to physical aspect of personality,

Though its relevance can't be discounted completely, even in maturity,

After all, senses know no sermons!

Yet there are other parameters of attraction too,

Naturalness, grace, common sense and modesty,

Generally makes a woman desirable,

Likewise, decency, manners, respectfulness and helpful nature,

Normally make men likeable,

Charm lies in rationality, sense of fairness and kindness,

Intellect, humility and humour add spice to it,

A bit of looks and aesthetic sense makes it complete, flawless,

A regular source of pleasure.

Obviously, there's no fixed rule or pattern,

Yet we can safely rely on these traits,

Some women, when they are young,

Go for worldly wisdom and street smartness,

When they age, their preferences change,

Now values and a loving heart become relevant,

Men, too, finally and with difficulty, rise above vital statistics,

And settle for a gentle smile and sweet nature.

So personality requires conscious effort,

A bit of grooming,

Conditioning of interior, refinement of exterior,

Few principles, too, with an easygoing, lighthearted spirit,

Consistent efforts for a purpose, yet detachment to the results,

Giving best to all relations, with bare minimum expectations,

An unshakeable faith in human positivity,

Besides, a bit of courage—

Courage to love and courage to introspect,

Acknowledgement without judgement, accepting people as they are,

Evolving with patience, with a calm approach,

Facing the world with a smile,

With an intent to contribute happiness to the world,

Seeking enlightenment, salvation and bonds eternal.

59. Promise

Silent emotions, disillusioned smile,

Industry despite tears, struggles without wile;

Courtesy despite devilish interior,

Artistic incline despite nonchalant exterior;

Impressive craft, creative longings,

Fertile intellect, charming musings;

Manly constitution, clear sight,

Sharp observation, conclusions and insight;

Laughter despite pain, entertaining company,

Academic rigour, intellectual alchemy;

Serious demeanour, fire within,

Equilibrium seen in a loss or a win;

Whenever I think of this new generation,

I feel a thrill, and a happy impulse pervades;

May God let loose many such promising kids,

And youths decide the complexion of coming decades.

60. Romance

I'm a teen of the 90s;

Grew up watching Bollywood movies;

We've seen the debut of all the kings and queens of Indian cinema;

Most of the movies then dealt with love and romance;

Innocently, most of us believed in such flimsy sentiments;

Frequently, we used to fall for looks, eyes, hair, voice, smile, etc.;

Mostly physical parameters;

Then we'd make an imaginary persona of the beloved;

And would fall head over heels without much prudence.

Even girls in those days seemed to be romantic;

Yet they were relatively mature;

They knew well that love is an illusive concept;

And life can't be supported by heart only;

On the contrary, boys would daydream;

Hover around girls' hostel and compromise with studies;

I was no exception;

Never missed a new movie;

Was more than eager to help female friends;

And entirely ignored studies;

Though, officially I was preparing for engineering entrance!

Later I realised my mistakes;

But as usual, wisdom came late to me;

Yet I don't regret my romantic adventures;

It had its own thrills, ecstasy and lessons.

Now when all issues are over;

I realise my immaturity;

Girls are, by nature, a bit practical;

They might be in love;

They may be romantically inclined;

Still, they can't ignore the reasons;

They are always aware of the pressures;

Of the family, friends and society;

It's convenient for them to compromise with the heart;

At least it was true in our time.

It's good to see that the time is changing;

Now girls are becoming independent;

And that's why the relation is on equal footing;

Friendship, compatibility and companionship are the priority;

Now personality of the candidate matters;

Money, family and status gradually losing relevance;

Arrange marriages are becoming obsolete;

Indian males are no longer the feudal masters;

They are caring, cooperative and friendly these days.

Presently, there is talk of matching 'vibe' & 'frequency';

Youngsters are disillusioned by love and its mystery;

It gives the heart a new hope of a possible chemistry;

But sadly, my youth is now a history.

61. Self-belief

Life is a tricky thing,

As human beings are a bit complex,

Supposedly a rational, sensitive creature,

Still, nature has made us all an animal,

Consequences are negativities,

Or toxicity as per youngsters' vocabulary,

Unsettling for us frequently,

Making fun of others, to mock in the guise of humour,

Personal remark crossing the boundary,

Expecting others to follow our lifestyle,

Arguments just for the sake of it,

Reminding us of our failures, academic as well as social,

Some samples of weakness of spirit or toxicity.

I need hardly say, it disturbs us,

Robs us of our tranquillity,

Poisons our happy solitude,

Reveals the distasteful, dark side of life,

Points out to the animality in all of us,

Demoralises & demotivates us,

And adds gloom to our already difficult life.

Despite this optimism is the preferred path to follow,

It's a deliberate choice, maybe a 'smart' choice,

As circumstances don't change as per our whims and fancies,

Only reaction to it is in our control,

So let's be positive and humane from our side,

Without expectations of reciprocity,

Let's not be affected by someone else's opinion,

Difficult at young age,

But gradually we may become immune to judgment,

After all, what is sacrosanct is our ' Self-belief',

There's no point in becoming vindictive,

Let karma do this ignoble work,

Let's just refine our own thoughts and actions,

Let's try to make 'our' life pleasing,

So just focus on brighter side of life,

In sum, just be optimistic,

Let's concentrate only on the merits of individuals,

It makes our life easy.

Self-belief is all about,

Giving priority to our own opinion about self,

Our own assessment matters,

Obviously, our genuine self-judgement,

No one knows us more than ourselves,

Actually, praise or criticism, both are inconsequential,

No doubt appreciation increases our confidence,

Yet we must assess its relevance,

Likewise, only few criticisms are valid; just ignore others,

In fact, the most difficult task in life is to protect ourselves,

To keep intact our self-esteem,

The world is desperately after it since childhood.

So fortify your inner self,

Surround yourself with positive people,

Just ignore the negative catalysts,

You can kill a giant by sheer indifference!

Learn this art, take it easy,

Try to be a lighthearted individual,

Life is a unique blend of positives and negatives,

Our choice of focus will decide,

Whether it's an unbearable obligation,

Or an interesting, beautiful journey,

Let there be an end to human travails,

And may the good sense prevail!

62. Knocking of Love

In the stillness of the night,

I lay motionless in my bed,

With my eyes closed, heart beating,

There is serenity—a calm tranquillity,

I receive an impulse, a calling!

Someone remembers me, a fervid longing.

Our minds interact, hearts talk,

It's a unique pleasant experience,

A rushing of blood; senses activated,

Soft kisses of the soul; passionate encounters,

The same, old, supernatural realm,

Some clarity of the eternity above,

Oh, this blissful knocking of love!

63. Grave Expectations

Expectations, the root of all heartbreaks,

The fountain of all possible pain!

You are loyal to someone,

Love might be your way of life, rather an emotion,

You may be helpful and friendly,

Warm and respectful to seniors, affectionate to juniors,

By and large fair and grounded, of sweet disposition,

Yet there is no guarantee of reciprocity of sentiments,

Just brace yourself for the dance of icy neutrality!

Refusals, cold responses, insensitivity and non-cooperation,

Disappointments galore, frequent letdowns,

Pain might be your destiny, always searching your address.

When I see the crowd flocking to temples,

And hear fine tunes for philanthropy,

And pious concerns for the underprivileged,

I'm amazed at the pervading insensitivity,

And the prevailing distaste for all human virtues,

As if God is a credulous child,

To be fooled by flowers and sweets.

Can a God-fearing person ever be a greedy brute?

Virtues seems to have only cosmetic significance,

An object of occasional fantasy,

To lighten a burdened conscience.

Yet I confess, Fault lies with me, not with others,

The people follow the principles they approve,

Nothing is right or wrong here, a thief or a saint equally justified,

All approaches have merits and demerits,

Calculations decide individual preference.

None of my business!

I try hard, very hard in fact,

To achieve such a state of mind,

Where expectations are non-existent,

A detached temper, a selfless soul,

Yet, as of now just a distant dream.

But I know, this is the prerequisite for continual happiness,

Actually, the human frailty comes in the way,

Only stones can be free from this soft noose called expectations! Sometimes I opine,

Hopefully, someday such spiritual excellence might come.

Still, in some silent corners of the world, you get love!

There is gratitude, friendly concern, fulfilling bonds,

Glances of warmth and respect, charming smiles, vital spirit,

Yes, it's there!

A pleasing assurance,

That despite the dark shadows, there is beauty in the world,

And despite being an arduous journey,

Life is always worth living.

64. The Experience...

I was in second year then,

A silent, shy boy in Hindu College,

Troubled by many issues,

Devastated by failures in engineering entrance,

There was pain of letting down parents and school teachers,

Trying to adjust emotionally to the modern, professional world,

Quite close to becoming cynical, almost an atheist,

After observing death, disease, poverty and inequality,

Thought God to be just an illusion, so stopped going to the temples,

And spent most of the time in pensive reflections.

I didn't have the maturity then,

To admire the beauty of the world,

And especially the beauty of human beings,

I couldn't realise, that men are full of flaws,

Yet they are studded with diamonds too,

With precious gems of fine qualities,

Having some uniqueness, blessed with the faculty of discretion,

And essentially appreciative of love & genuineness.

As I was troubled by many questions and confusion, I'd read a lot,

And would also think with my limited youthful intellect,

Trying to decode men, women, life and success,

Confidence, personality, culture and religion,

And definitely the presence or absence of God,

Striving all the time to eliminate the faults of my nature,

Particularly sentimentality and vehemence,

I had heard the story of Buddha in childhood,

And he seemed to be the role model,

'Be your own light' or 'Self-reliance' used to be the guiding light.

One day, I was sitting quietly in a playground during vacation,

Some kids were playing cricket; I was just watching them,

Parallelly lost in my own thoughts,

Suddenly I experienced a sweet explosion!

In between the eyes, the place marked for a 'Third Eye',

As per our Hindu religious beliefs,

I couldn't understand what was happening,

At that time, I didn't even know about 'Self-realisation',

As I was hardly religious then,

Even today, I'm a non-believer in rituals,

So, it was an ecstatic upliftment of mind,

It seemed that I was floating in the universe,

Suddenly a voice told me, 'Monarch of the three worlds',

Again, I didn't know what the three worlds are,

Yet what a blissful feeling it was!

Absolute pleasure; far superior to those of the senses,

A pure intellectual kick and a thrilling delight!

I sat there for three hours in that blissful state; I forgot everything,

I felt as if I was connected to a supreme being sitting above,

And I was trying to find out the meaning of the whole experience.

Suddenly I realised,

My family members might be worried, so I thought of
returning home,

Many things happened later, not an easy experience at all,

Perhaps the most difficult situation a boy might face!

Time's beats in the ear, and death staring in the eye,

Test of will-power and fortitude,

Self-realisation demanding its price!

Sacrifice the life dear, was the call.

Naturally, it couldn't be accepted, so the fight begins.

Victor, after a fortnight!

Man becoming time, rapid changes in time's scale,

Past, present and future losing relevance,

Realising man is just a puppet in the circular time,

Futility of the material world,

Age—just a number in larger scheme of things.

And then the encounter!

A Godly being in human shape,

Who was he?

Almighty, God, Father or the Creator?

Precise answer I can't give,

Sometimes faith is above rationality,

But I was scared; something, somewhere is wrong,

I just closed my eyes.

But how soothing this experience was!

To know that there is a Ruler, an Almighty or God,

Is so relieving, so calming, so assuring,

Life is eternal, endless, perpetual,

We're just in this world of transition for the time being,

And as God is a reality, there is supremacy of karma,

All debts will be paid someday,

And however tough life might be,

It will always be beautiful.

65. Time & Love

Enlightenment by chance,

And a chance meeting with the Almighty!

It was not premeditated;

Maybe falling in love and continence are the reasons,

Entirely God's blessings!

But it comes with the tests,

These tests are supernatural in nature.

Death awaits with its snares,

So will-power summoned to face it;

It was difficult, yet defeated death somehow,

Then comes 'Responsibility of Time';

Create it for posterity!

But first division of time in moments,

Differentiation and integration was the key;

Instantaneous decisions taken!

Seconds divided into moments,

Four moments to be precise,

Task, in fact, a difficult task,

Completed with God's blessings.

Now another challenge awaiting,

There is a concept of 'Female Time';

For some unknown reason,

They have always been harsh to me;

So now a long battle waiting: eternal struggle,

Perennial quest for power!

You love a girl, and she becomes powerful,

Obviously, in supernatural sense,

Ideally, their loyalty should be to her lover,

But somehow, it has never been in my case;

Yet, 'not giving up' is my decision,

'No coward soul is mine' as Emily Bronte said,

Naturally, there is disillusionment regarding romance.

Sometimes a voice comes from within,

You have had the choice, sweetheart;

To play this 'Game of Love' sensibly,

You know what you've chosen and done;

Someday the tables may turn,

And I might call the shots;

Rest assured, darling,

You've started this sinister 'Game of Love,

I'll finish it to sweet finality.

66. Happiness

Sufficient money for a comfortable survival;

Mental peace and calm;

Contentment in heart and sound sleep;

Few principles, purpose, efforts and hope;

Clarity about men, women and life;

Freedom from conflict, inner as well as outer;

Continence, temperance and rational desires.

A soul free from negativity and cynicism;

Tolerance for fellow human beings;

Minimal weight upon conscience;

A bit of humility, a bit of forgiveness;

Avoiding & ignoring judgement and assessment;

Something to read and think.

An eye for the beauty of the world;

An engaged mind; sweet disposition;

Not taking oneself seriously, just work with sincerity;

Some skills to be confident of;

Some achievements to be proud of;

A profession as per the temperament;

A hobby beyond the profession.

Few people who love you;

Few friends who like you;

A partner who accepts and respects you;

A bit of romance and humour;

Physical intimacy as per the appetite.

Some spiritual wisdom;

Some insight about the supernatural realm;

Belief in God if not the knowledge;

Some intimation about immortality;

And possibility of an eternal soulmate.

It's a tall order;

Naturally happiness, by and large, is a mirage;

Yet we've free will too;

Which makes it majorly a conscious choice.

67. Princess Charming

Sensitive eyes, pleasing smile and dusky clouds of hair;

Appealing voice, the blazing glow and the feminine air;

I confess, lovely ladies, these are ammunition enough,

To accelerate our heartbeat's flow;

Indeed, these weapons get you attention;

Though necessary, not enough for admiration!

What else, do you morons, further expect from us?

Comes the obvious complaint!

Wait a bit, Madame, I'll quickly explain;

After all, it's an interesting terrain!

Temperate vivacity with social intelligence;

Sobriety ladies and a bit of aesthetic sense;

Natural expressions, little bit of diligence;

Warm, fleeting gaze, soothing fragrance;

Talkative temperament, a bit of silence;

Attach to you all, madams, disarming elegance!

Love, yes love, fascinates boys' imagination;

As loyalty stems from these considerations;

Heart demands equality, dislikes submission;

And perhaps it is a rational expectation;

Lively companionship and the spice of romance;

A universal wish, whether India or France!

I know, quest of perfection is wishful thinking;

We have some blessings; few traits might be missing;

Just acceptance and commitment with an attitude loving;

Makes you all damsels, a Princess Charming!

68. Pursuit of Excellence

When conscience is shocked

And heart travails;

When emotions freeze

And silence prevails;

When righteousness is annihilated

And reality knocks;

When promise disappoint

And society mocks;

When mind judges the heart

And affection succumbs to mockery;

When poverty germinates disdain

And character realises its futility;

When friends disappear

And loneliness lingers;

When relations vanish

And confidence is in danger;

A divine fire possesses the soul

Which redefines the being on the whole;

Passion and patience have a commanding presence

And heart announces pursuit of excellence!

69. Success & Excellence

Success is social, excellence individual,

One can achieve excellence, still he can be a failure,

A person might be a success, still be lacking in excellence,

An artist might have brilliance,

Yet he needs social acknowledgement to become a success.

Now what's the right attitude?

The best strategy?

Here is my take...

Don't be in a haste to succeed,

Still don't waste too much time on excellence,

Perfectionism is a kind of malady,

Strike a balance between these two,

Success is always preferable,

After all, man is a social animal,

A man who fails is defeated on all fronts,

As a son, a brother, as a friend or a lover,

Yet excellence should also be a concern.

You might have some dormant potential,

Some latent art; seek for this and explore possibilities,

A bit of introspection, a bit of self-analysis,

Who knows, some grand success might be awaiting you.

So success is society, excellence beauty,

Success is power, excellence pleasure,

Success is monetary, excellence repute,

Success is magnitude, excellence altitude,

Success is possession, excellence salvation,

Success is affluence, excellence influence,

Success is glamorisation, excellence self-realisation,

Finally, success is recognition, excellence ammunition!

Hence, let there be success with excellence.

70. Love at First Sight

When our eyes first met,

I was in a world of fantasy,

When you looked at me,

I was thrown into ecstasy,

When your name sounded the sweetest,

And your face was a delicacy,

It was love at first sight,

Love at first sight,

Love at first sight.

When the message was silently conveyed,

And there was nothing left to say,

When I waited for you,

And there was love night and day,

When I was anxious for a glimpse of you,

And there was thrill in the heat of May,

It was love at first sight,

Love at first sight,

Love at first sight.

Now when I'm alone,

I think of you,

I doubt sometimes,

But hope my love is true,

Indeed, I'm in love with you,

Of yours, I've no clue,

Yet dear, it's Love at first sight,

Love at first sight,

Love at first sight.

71. Reading

There was a long vacation recently;

After 4-5 years for me;

Generally, I prefer to read in holidays;

But, somehow, I wasn't in a mood to do so this time;

Actually, I got disillusioned with books and reading;

I remembered how passionately;

I was attached to reading during college time;

All my little savings would go for books;

Fiction and non-fiction;

Science and arts;

Poetry, plays and philosophy;

And the autobiographies!

But what have these books given me?

Nothing, absolutely nothing...

Thus, I reflected;

So, I decided not to read them this vacation;

Spent most of my time on Instagram, Facebook and YouTube;

Took subscription of all the OTT platforms;

Watched many pointless movies;

Just slept or lay on the bed lazily;

Nothing to do with books!

But very soon got fed up with all these diversions;

Felt some kind of vacancy and disequilibrium;

A kind of uneasiness, stress and inertia.

Naturally, I was forced to think about the only alternative, my books;

They reminded me of the time when I first read them;

How intellectually stimulating some of them were!

Promising me hope and ambitions;

Shaping my personality and sense of language;

Removing my self-doubts and confusion;

Giving me some kind of understanding;

Of my society and surroundings;

Refining my perception about the multiplicity of human sentiments;

Friendship and love, relationships and family, culture and religion;

God and destiny, self-realisation and death.

So once again I was attracted to my books;

I could feel my loving attachment to them;

I decided to have a relook at them;

Yes, in material sense they may have been ineffectual;

Yet these books were not entirely useless;

If nothing, at least they give me company;

My friends in my perpetual solitude;

A kind of interaction with great minds of the past;

So once again I took refuge in dear books;

In the familiar company.

Once again, I was in sync with my soul,

At peace with myself;

Calm, tranquil and on the path of self-discovery;

Searching for the answers I couldn't find;

Of life, love, death and immortality;

Of God, karma, and bonds eternal;

After all, when all relations succumb to misgivings;

I'm left only with the faithful company of my books.

72. Mothers

When I'm alone,

And reflect on the tests and trials of life,

Only one picture comes to my mind,

As a sheltering tree,

A constant in flux,

I've seen the changing dynamics of all relationships,

But there is one relation,

Which never changes,

Thank heaven for that!

I've seen her sacrifices,

For the family, for the kids,

Without ever demanding anything, without any complaint,

Somewhere I read,

God can't be everywhere,

That's why we have mother,

And how true!

When we're heartbroken,

When we face the stings of failure,

When the heat of life is too much to bear,

There's only one embrace we look for,

Mothers are God's sweetest blessing,

Loving, caring and full of tender feelings!

73. A Father

I love my kids,

especially daughters;

With sons, I'm a bit strict,

Actually, there is a concern for discipline;

After all, life is not a cakewalk,

And I've to train them for it;

But with the daughters, I'm a bit indulgent,

Sometimes I try to be tough with them;

But generally, I give in to their demands,

I find their manners, love and smile so disarming;

I simply become helpless,

Besides, I know someday they'll go;

To a new home as per the custom,

So, I become a bit lenient;

Slowly, I'm preparing myself for that day.

I love my wife and my relatives,

I still care for my siblings and my friends;

But somehow most of my time and energy,

Is consumed in providing for my family;

I'm a bit reluctant to express my love,

As I've been taught, men should be reserved;

Sometimes I'm misunderstood,

People think I'm not sensitive;

But this is not so,

My kids too seem to be closer to their mother,

Mostly, she gets the hugs, the cajoling and cuddling,

I don't mind;

Yet sometimes I feel the distance, the coldness.

Despite all, I maintain my silence, my gravity, my calm;

After all, I've to prepare my kids for life,

I've to make them men and women of my choosing;

A man loving and respectful to women,

A woman kind and caring to men;

An asset not only for family but for society,

They are my hope, my ambition,

Hopefully, someday they'll make me proud;

This is my only wish, my regular prayer,

Like others, I'm just an ordinary father.

74. Lessons from Cricket

Finally, India won the World Cup,

What a thrilling match!

Ecstasy, heartbeat, palpitations, hope, and then victory!

Klaasen and Miller almost took the match away from us,

But, then a brilliant catch by SKY,

And we were back into the game,

A nail-biting finish!

Our heroes rose to the occasion,

And gifted the country the World Cup.

We all have played cricket in our teens,

Some of us must have been mad after it,

Before being thrown into the bottomless pit of academics,

Indeed, it's a beautiful game,

And has taught me many important lessons...

First thing, you can't sit back on your past laurels,

Every match is a new match!

Stats are useless,

Past and future both are irrelevant,

Learn from the past and move on,

Only the present matters,

You might be a school topper,

But the college is a different ball game,

Era of competition starts now,

So don't be complacent,

Keep giving your best.

Like cricket, victory and defeat is part and parcel of life,

There's no point in being euphoric in victory,

And depressed in defeat,

Equanimity is a useful virtue,

The middle path of Buddha.

Further, match is not finished till the last ball,

So it is with life,

Years of failure,

Then one good academic result,

And the table turns!

No one knows when comes the success,

So, keep fighting, keep struggling,

Till the last breath.

Then the team spirit,

One swallow doesn't make a summer,

Business, politics, cinema, sports or institution,

For anything big, you need a team,

So learn how to get along with the people.

And then, like cricket life is a battle of nerves,

A perpetual sine curve,

With regular troughs and peaks,

Keep your cool when the going gets tough,

Turbulence will subside gradually.

Finally, and most importantly, the relevance of destiny,

Game changes in the blink of an eye,

One good over or a couple of wickets,

Everything changes,

So be grounded, be humble;

Eyes to the star but feet always on the ground,

Youth tells us the supremacy of efforts,

Age tells us the role of chance,

South Africa played well, yet the cup was not in their destiny,

We've to accept what comes our way,

After all, however smartly we play,

God is still the only player!

75. The Farewell

Recently there was farewell of the final-year students,

All the juniors gave a warm adieu to their seniors,

The seniors too bade an emotional goodbye,

I was also part of one such function,

The Farewell of Commerce Students.

I've not taught the final year students of commerce in DCAC till now,

Yet I could relate to the solemn air,

As I've taught one of the passing out batches,

The Economics final year,

I taught them a GE paper,

Lovely boys and girls,

A batch of variety and contrasts,

Bright, enthusiastic, fun-loving and interesting,

And majority well-mannered and decent,

Now they are graduating,

Needless to say, they'll miss the college life.

Their farewell reminds me of my own.

It was one of the sad moments of my life,

How badly I miss those days!

The carefree, easy and interesting college life,

When life was a continual fun,

Humour, laughter and lots of puns,

Full of energy, youth and wit,

A life of dreams, hope and grit,

Academic concerns, anxiety of exams,

Multiplicity of crushes and their charms!

When college ends, there is a sense of loss,

Life later may be beautiful, or may go for a toss,

Work and finance absorb your time,

Serious you become, however soothing the climes,

Now you behave, as becomes a grown-up,

Grace and calm are your expected make-up.

There is hardly a suggestion to these passing out students,

Just a wish that your life, be free of all impediments,

Never lose faith, despite the strife,

There is beauty and charm, in all phases of life,

New friends, new relations, a new place awaits you,

Your college, your teachers and your juniors will miss you!

- Vikas Kumar